COOL DINOSAUR

COPY COLORING BOOK FOR KIDS

This book belongs to

____

____

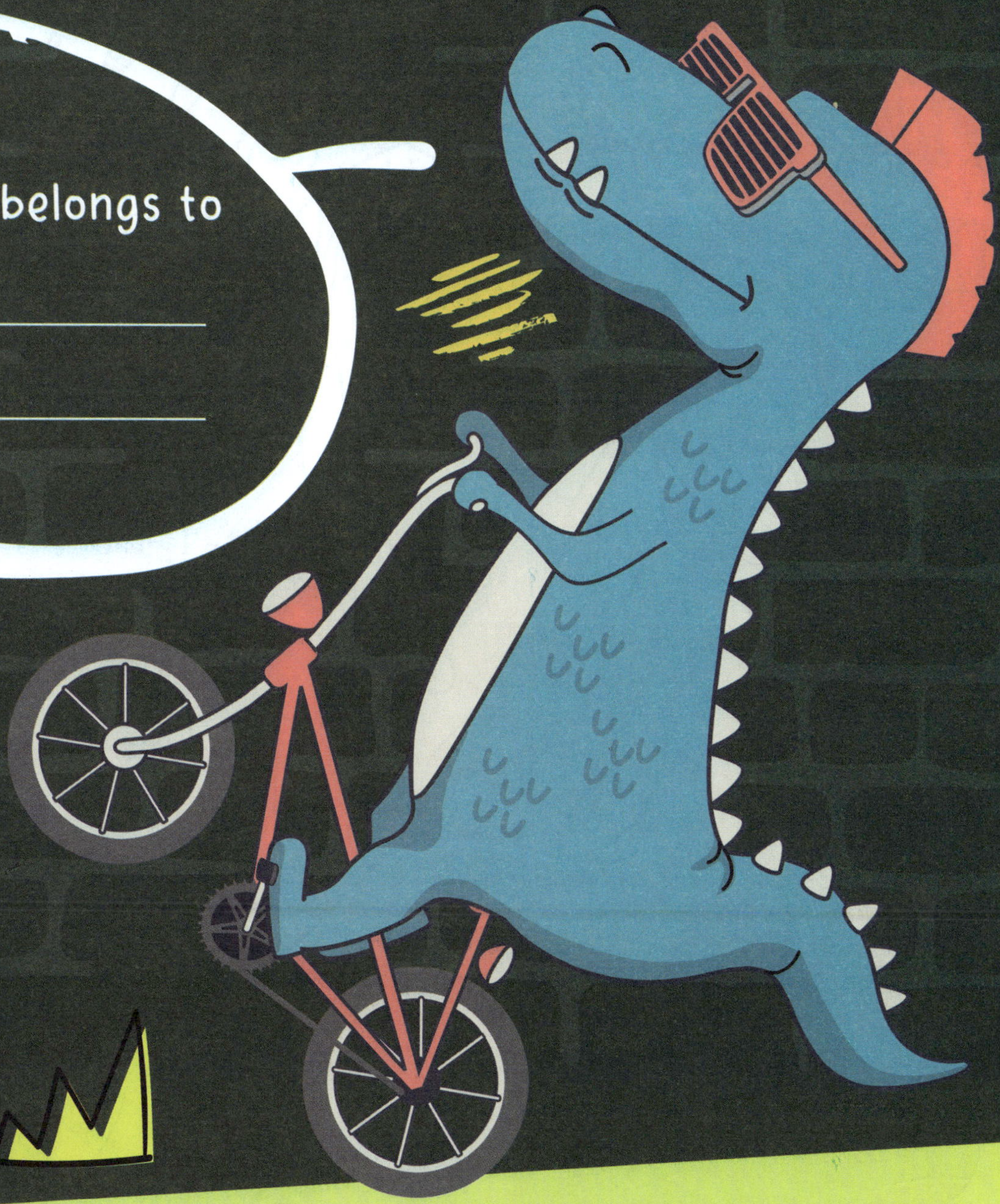

Wonder House

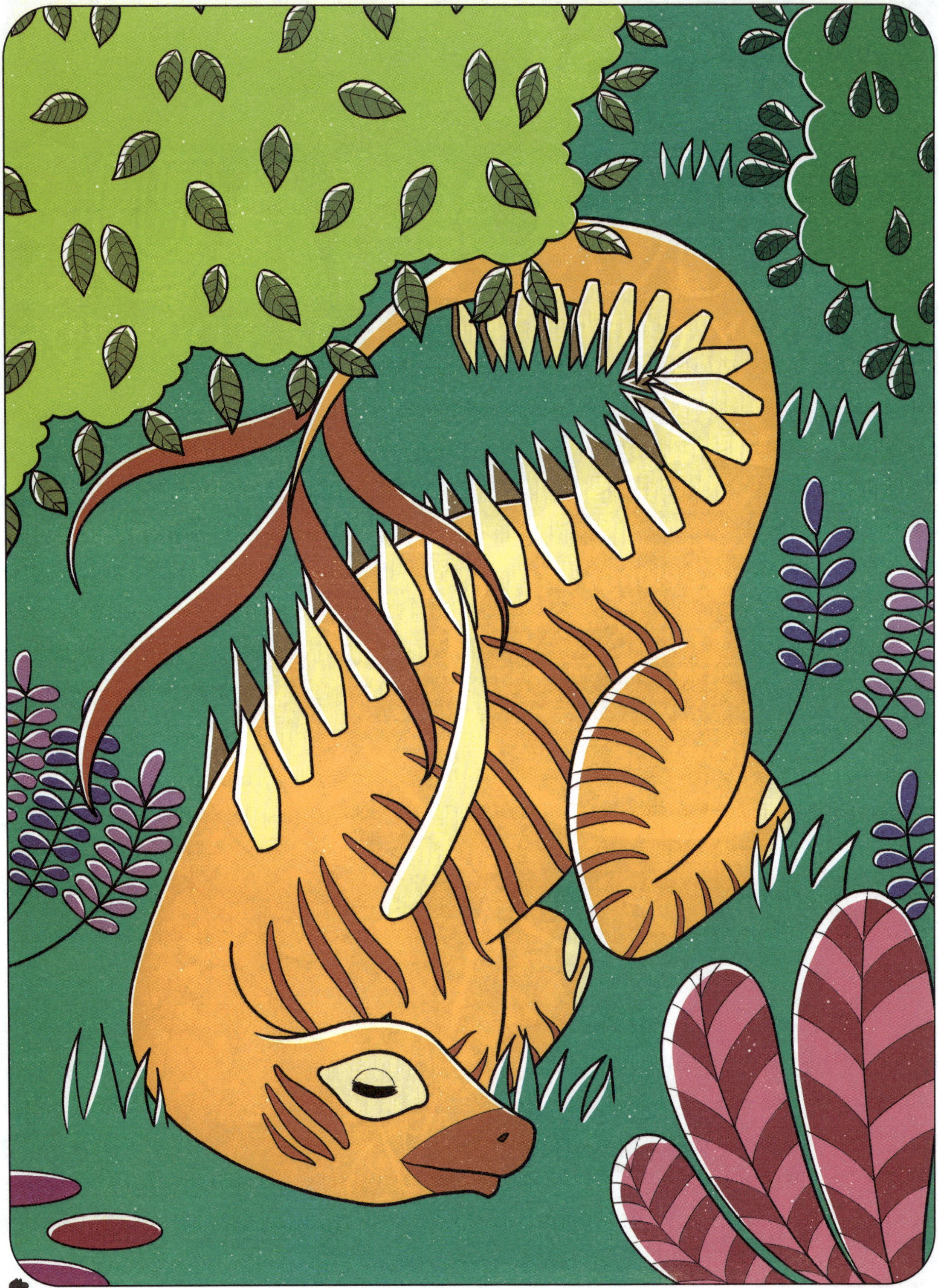

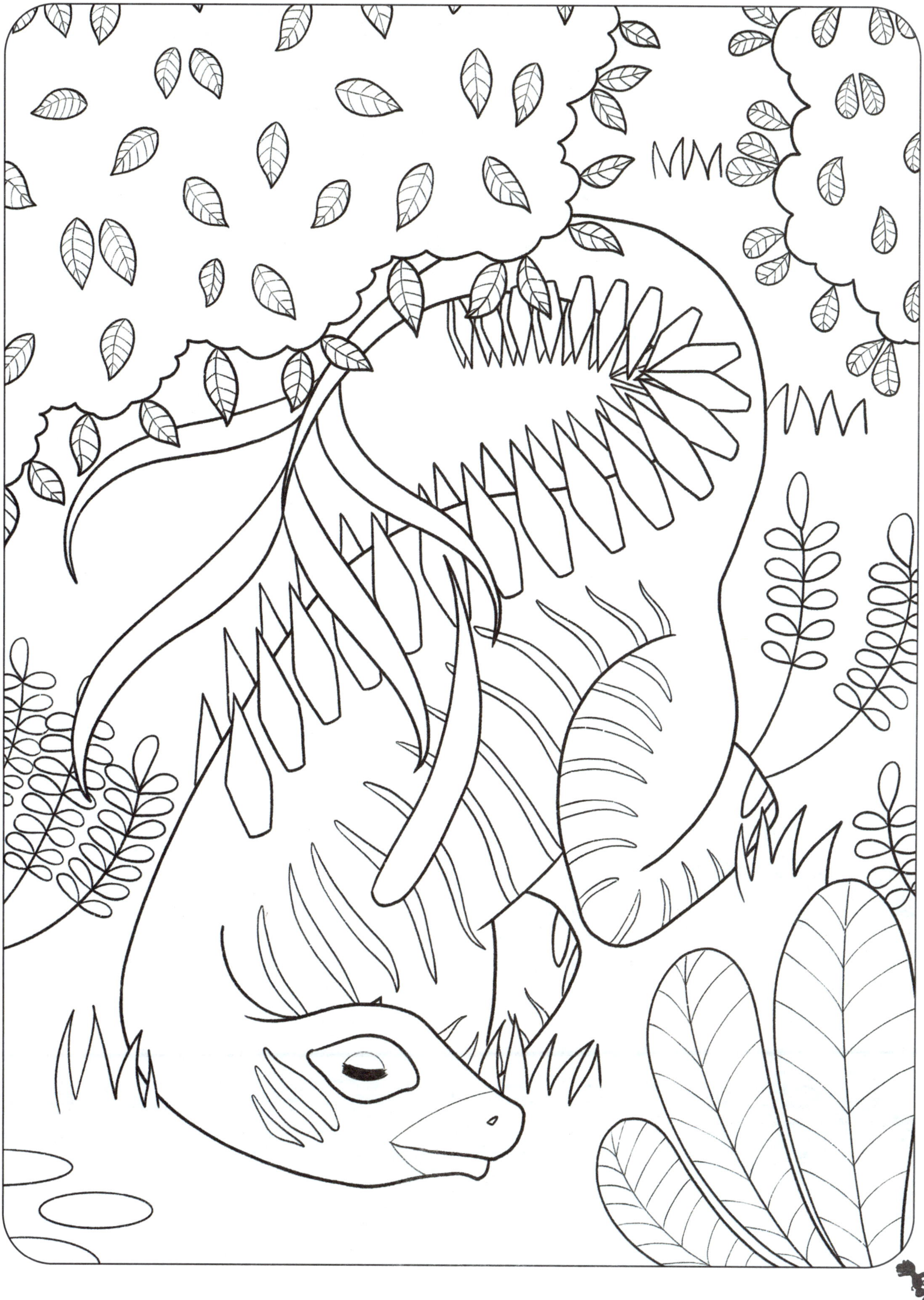

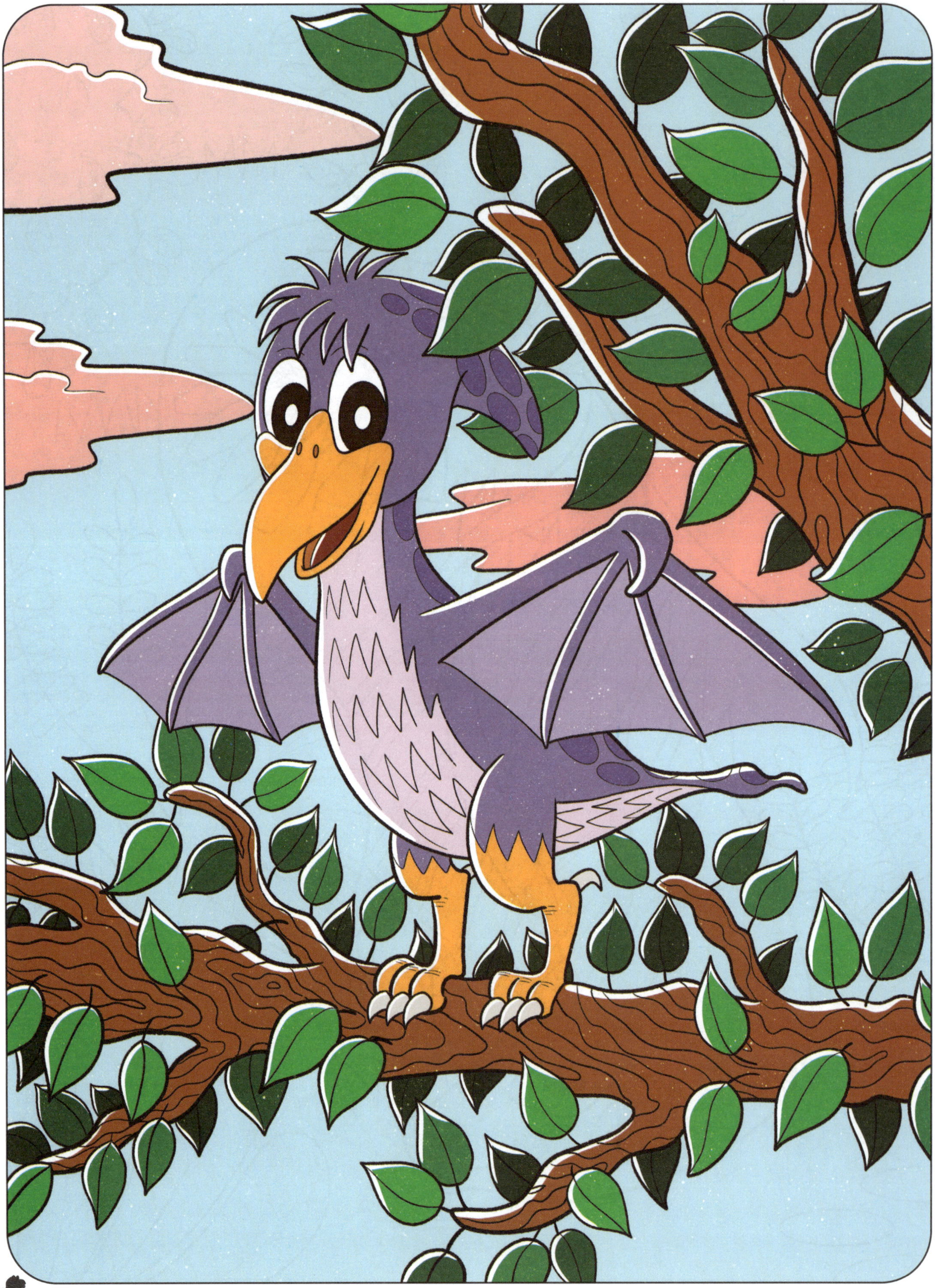

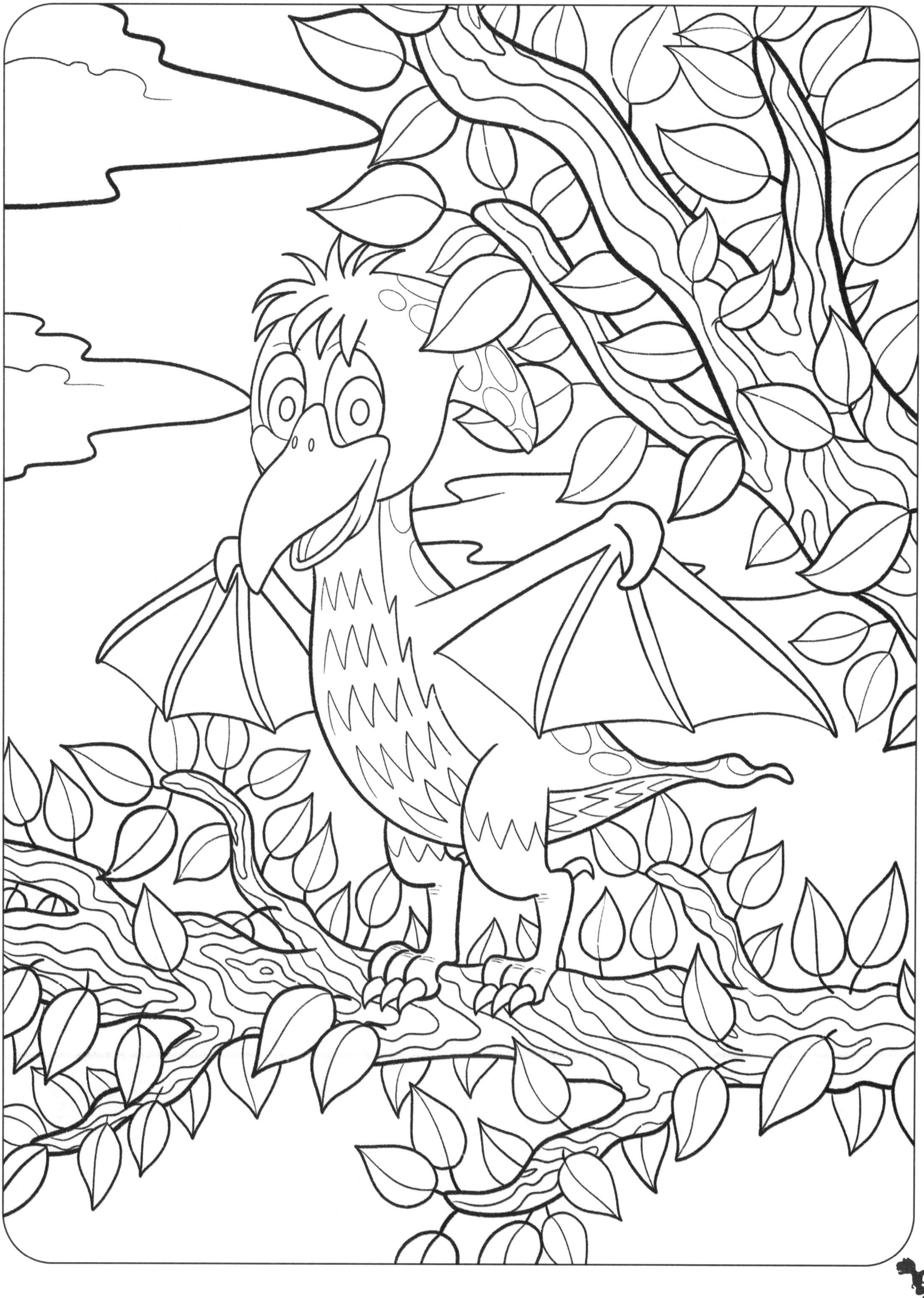

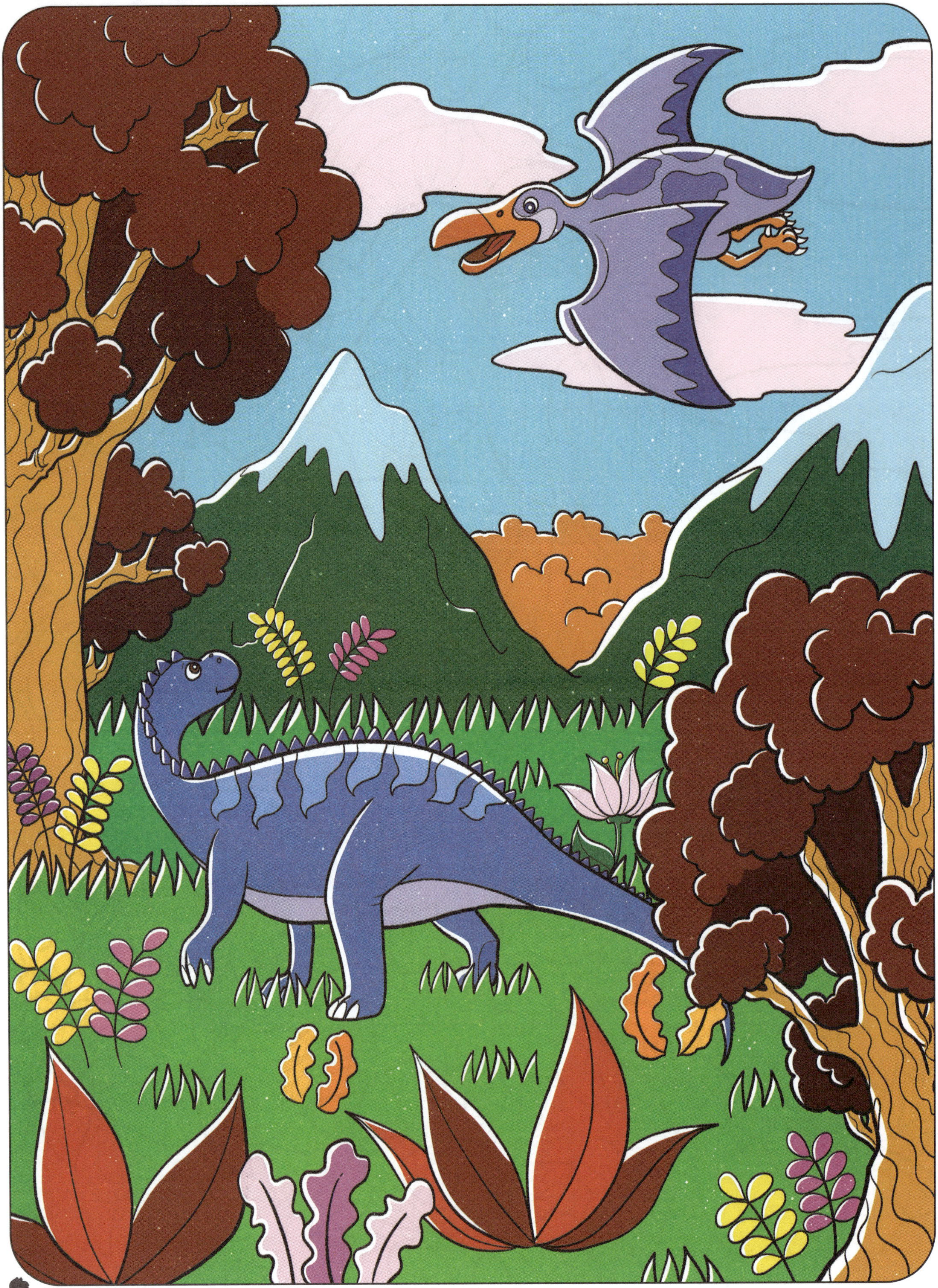

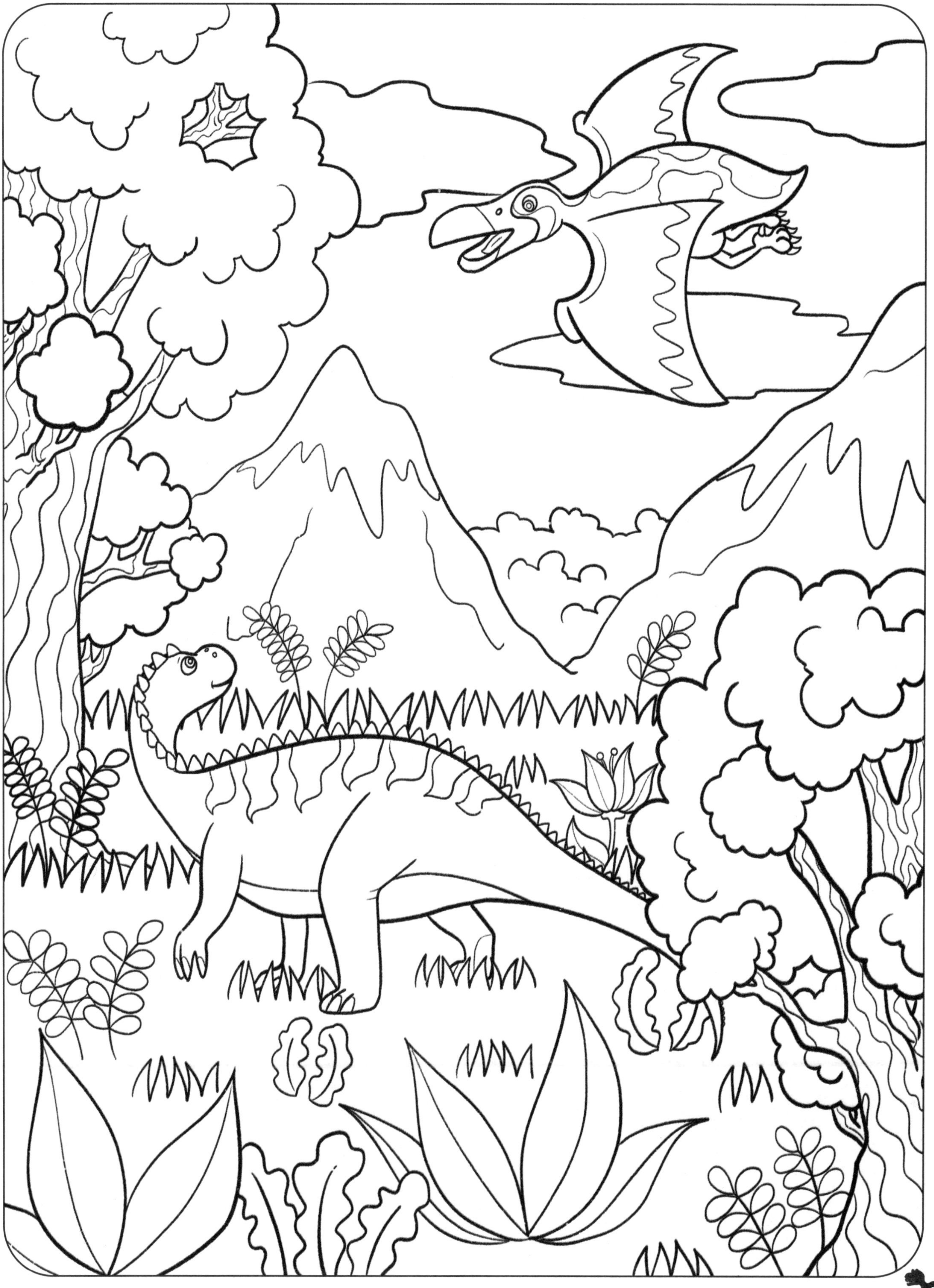

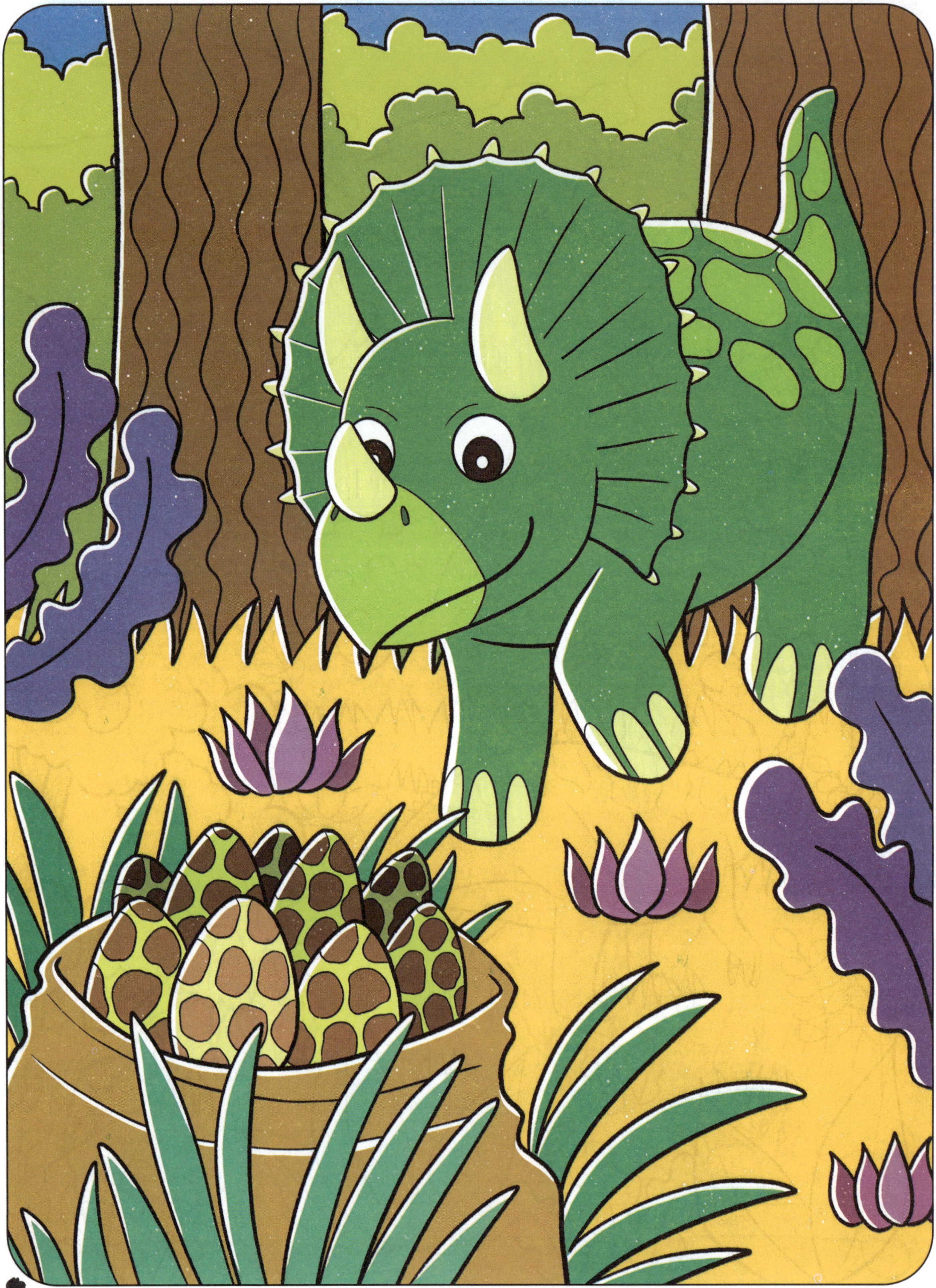

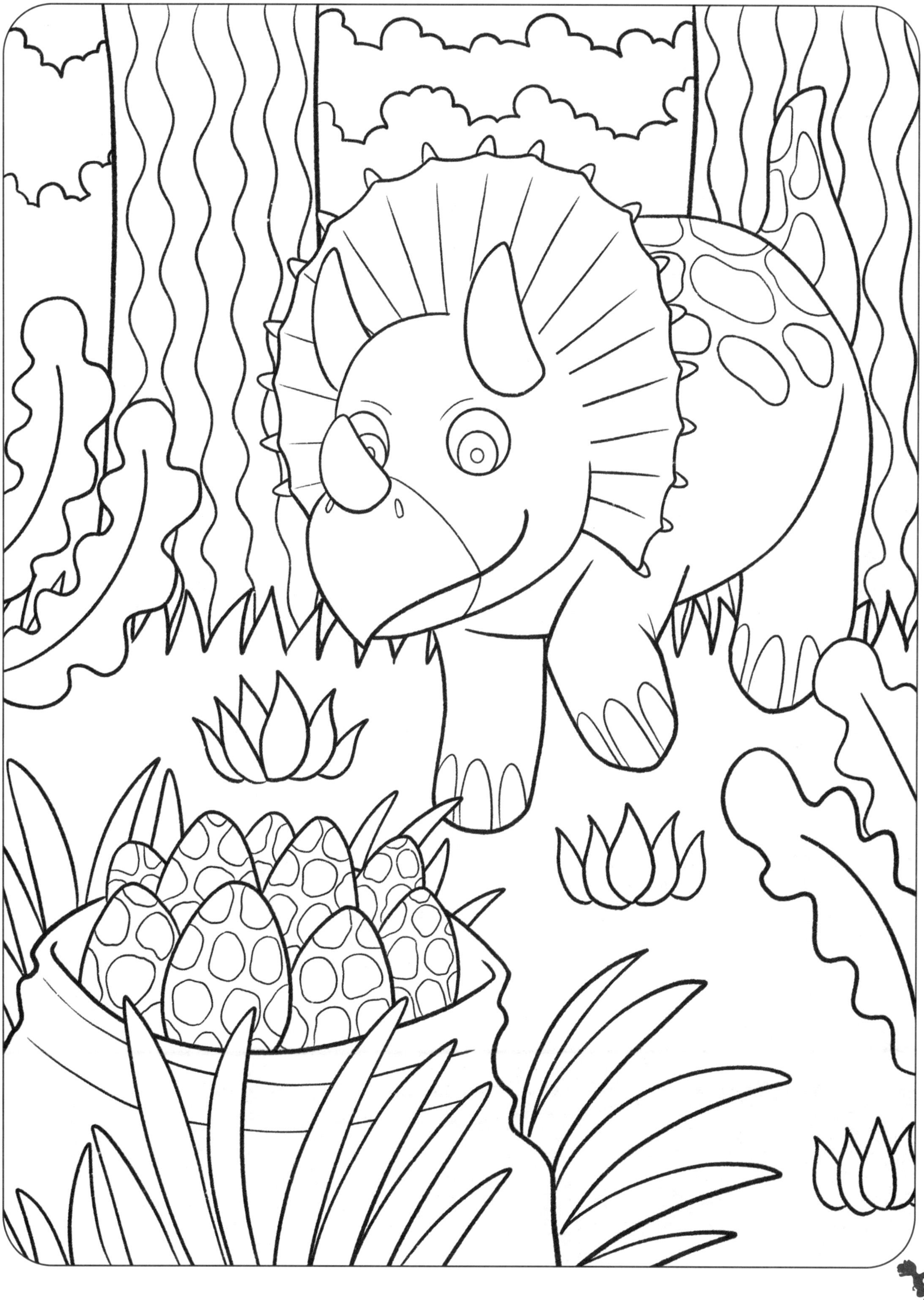

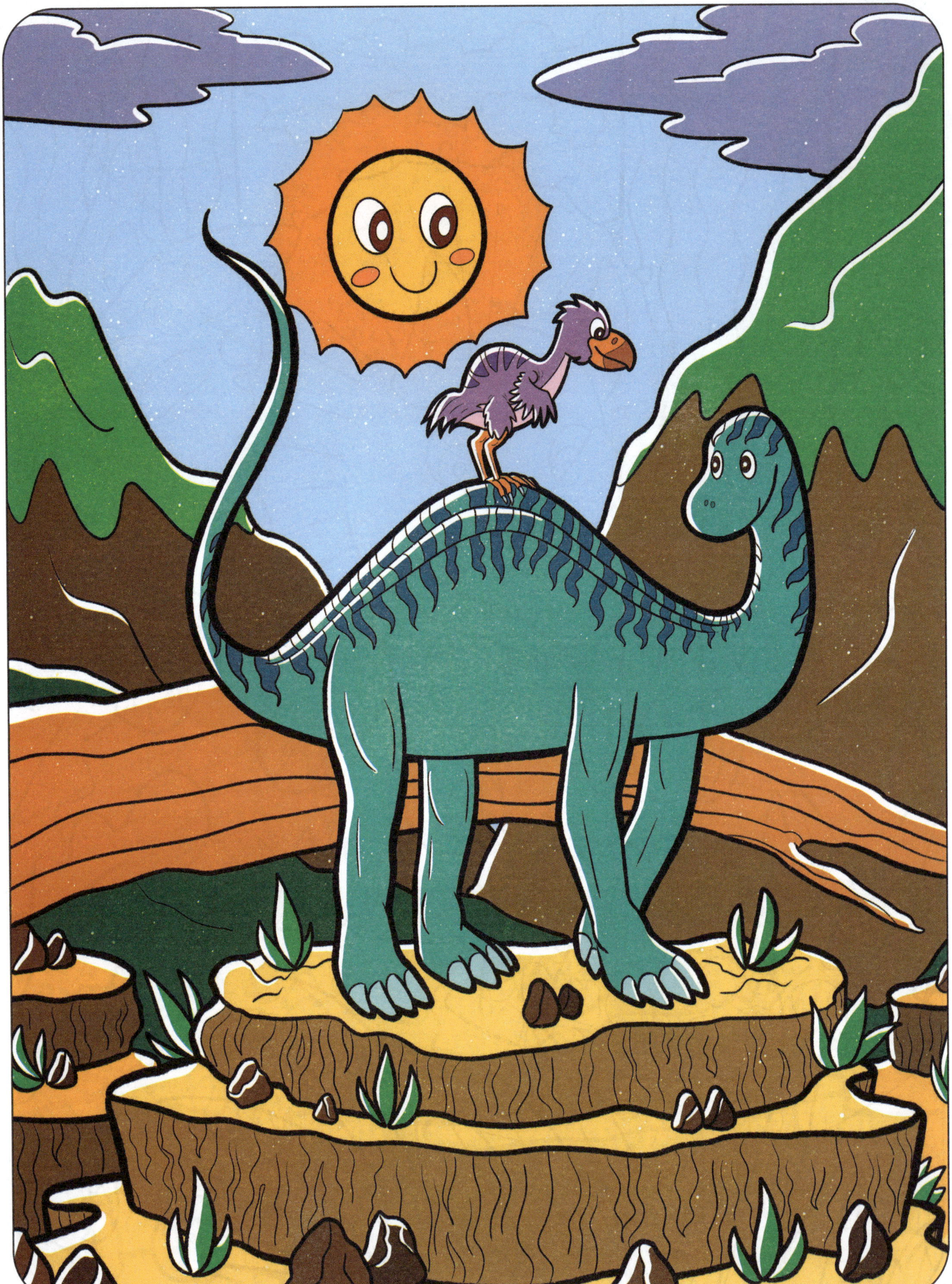

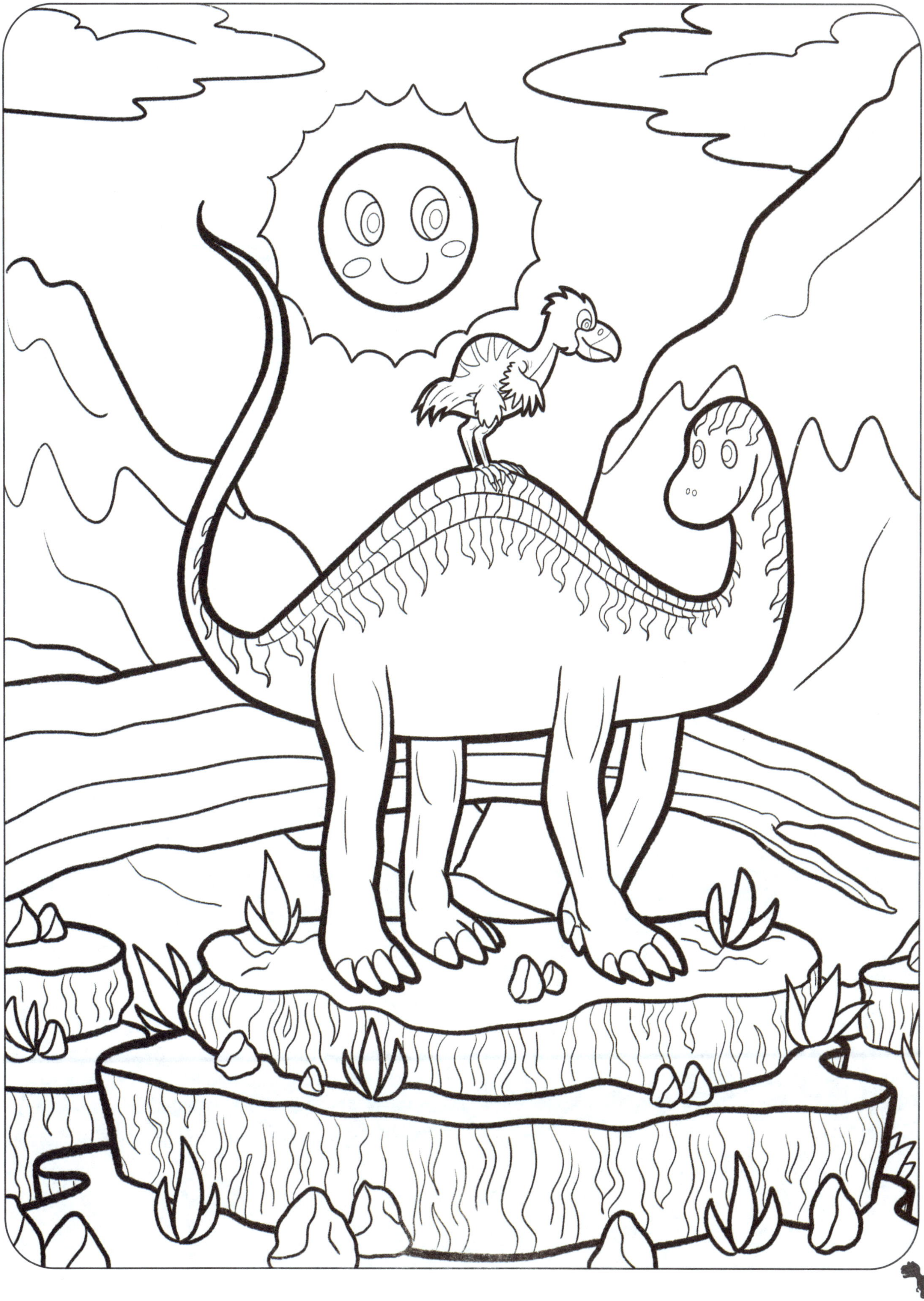

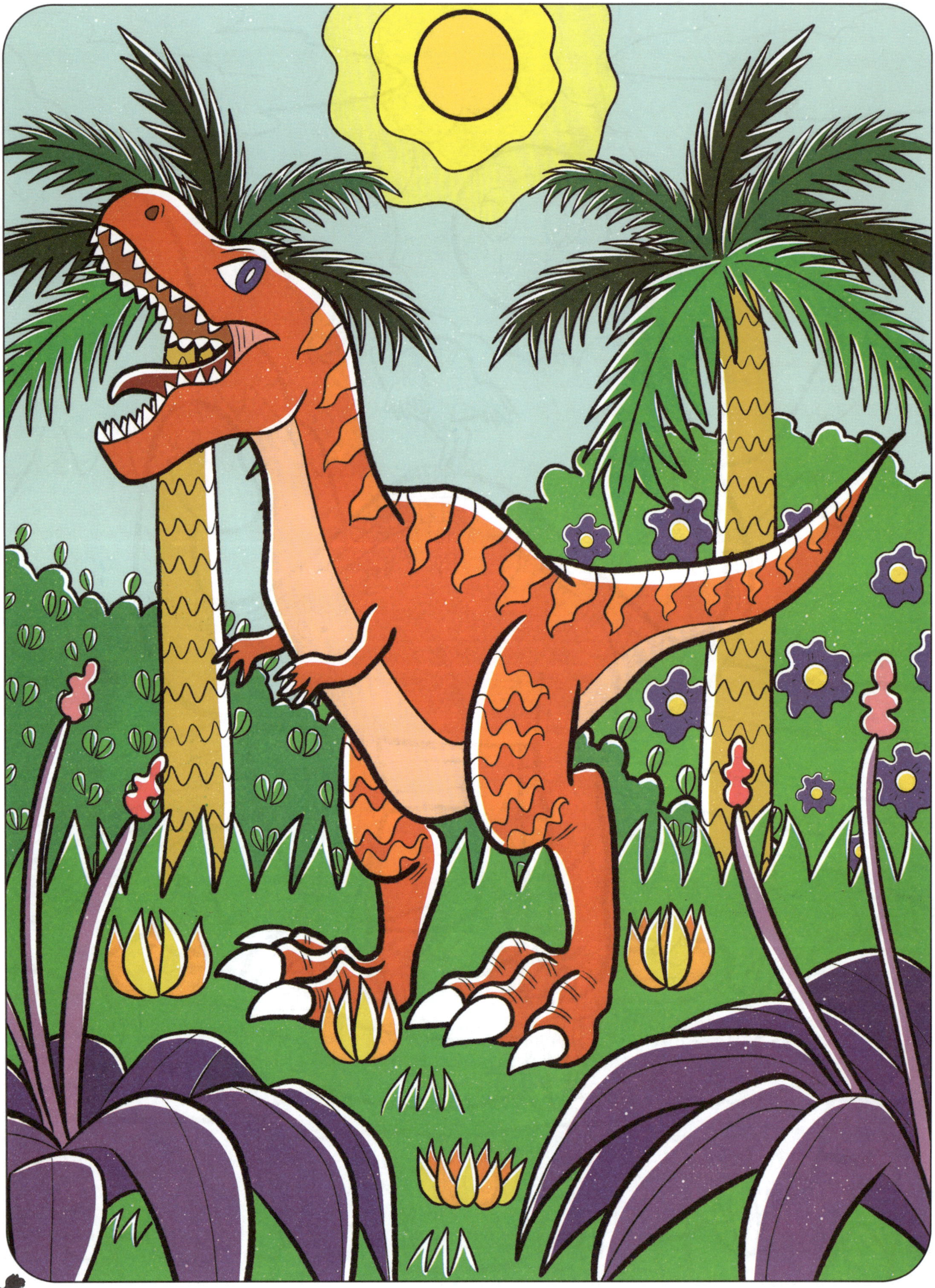

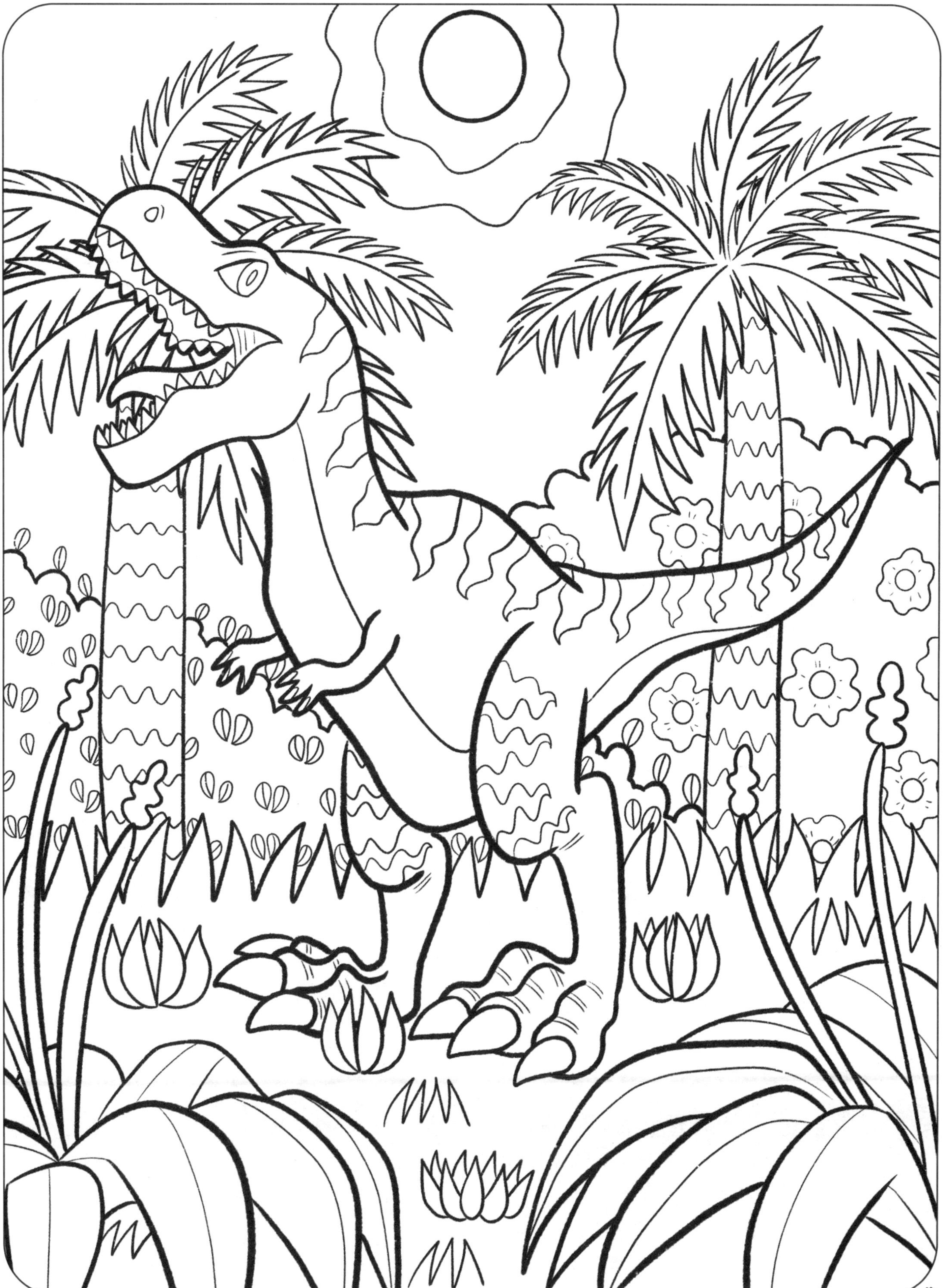

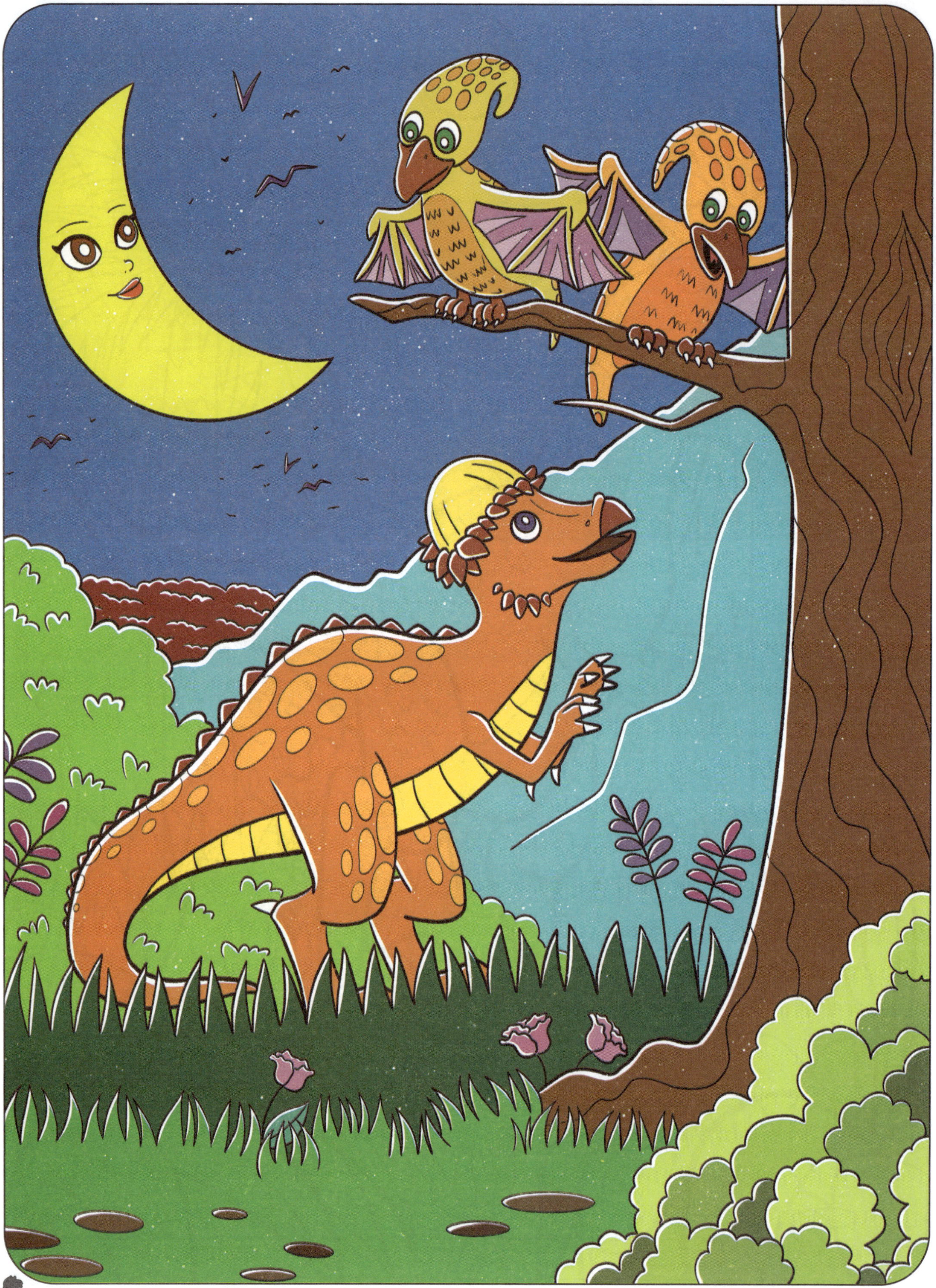

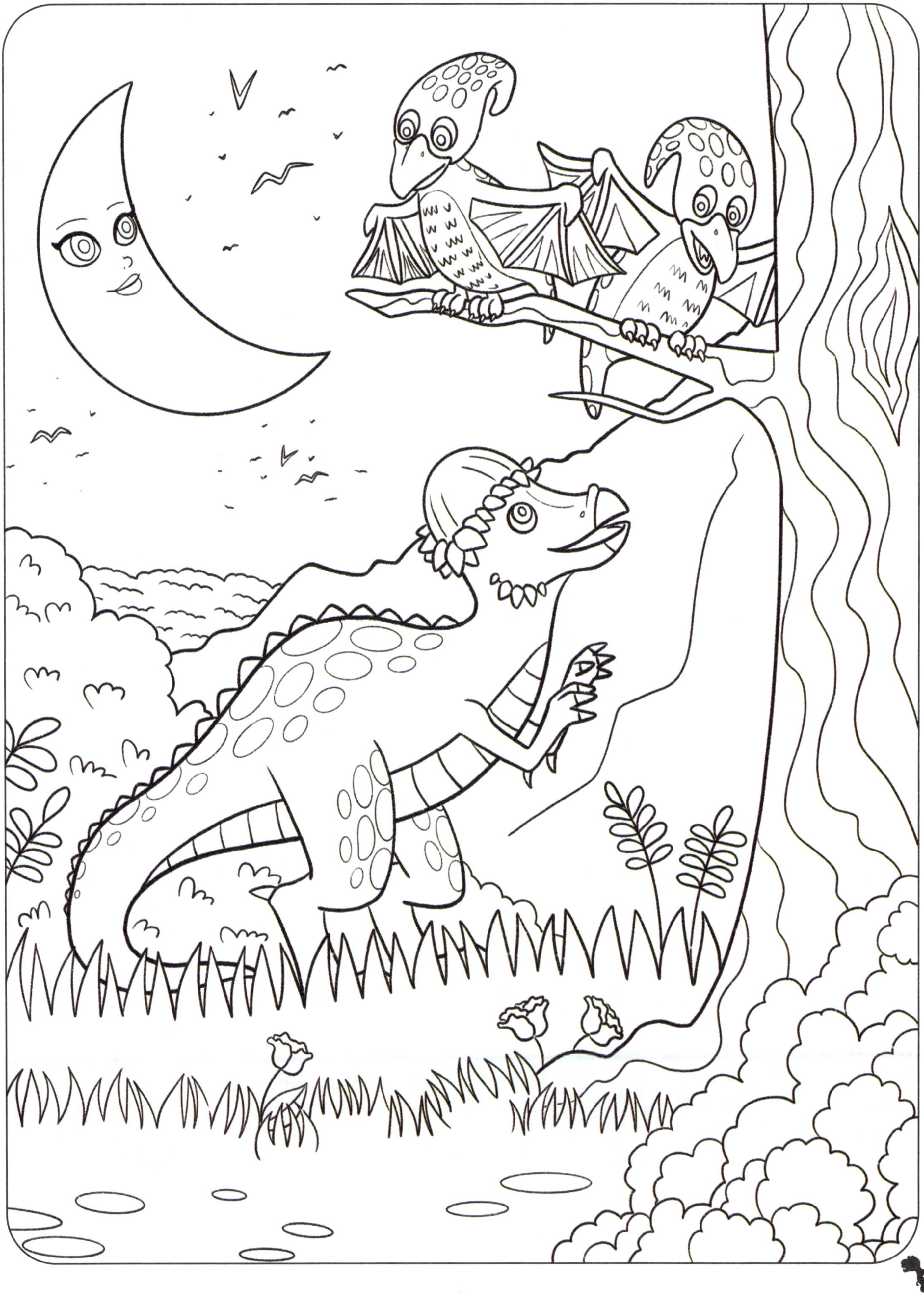

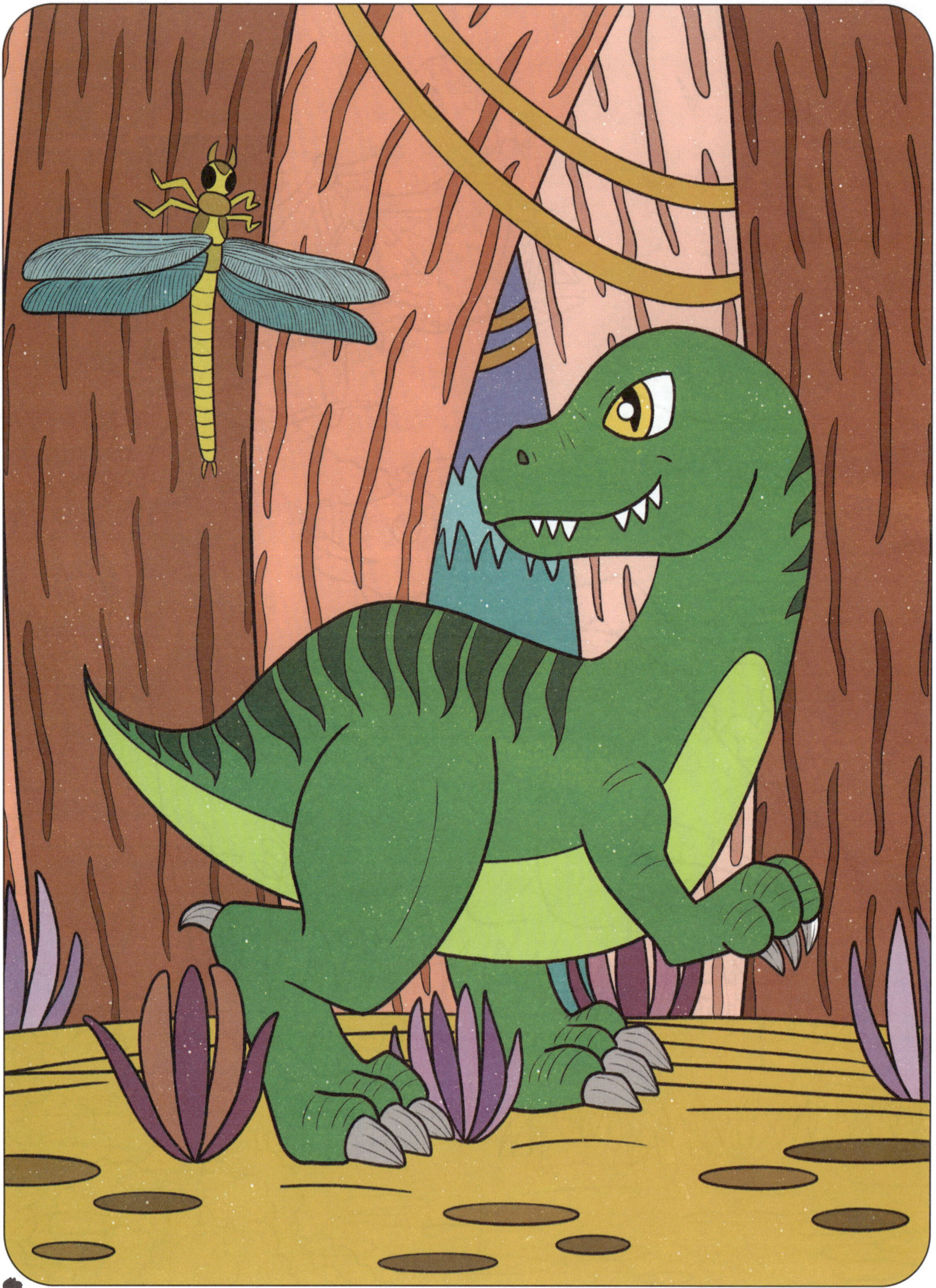

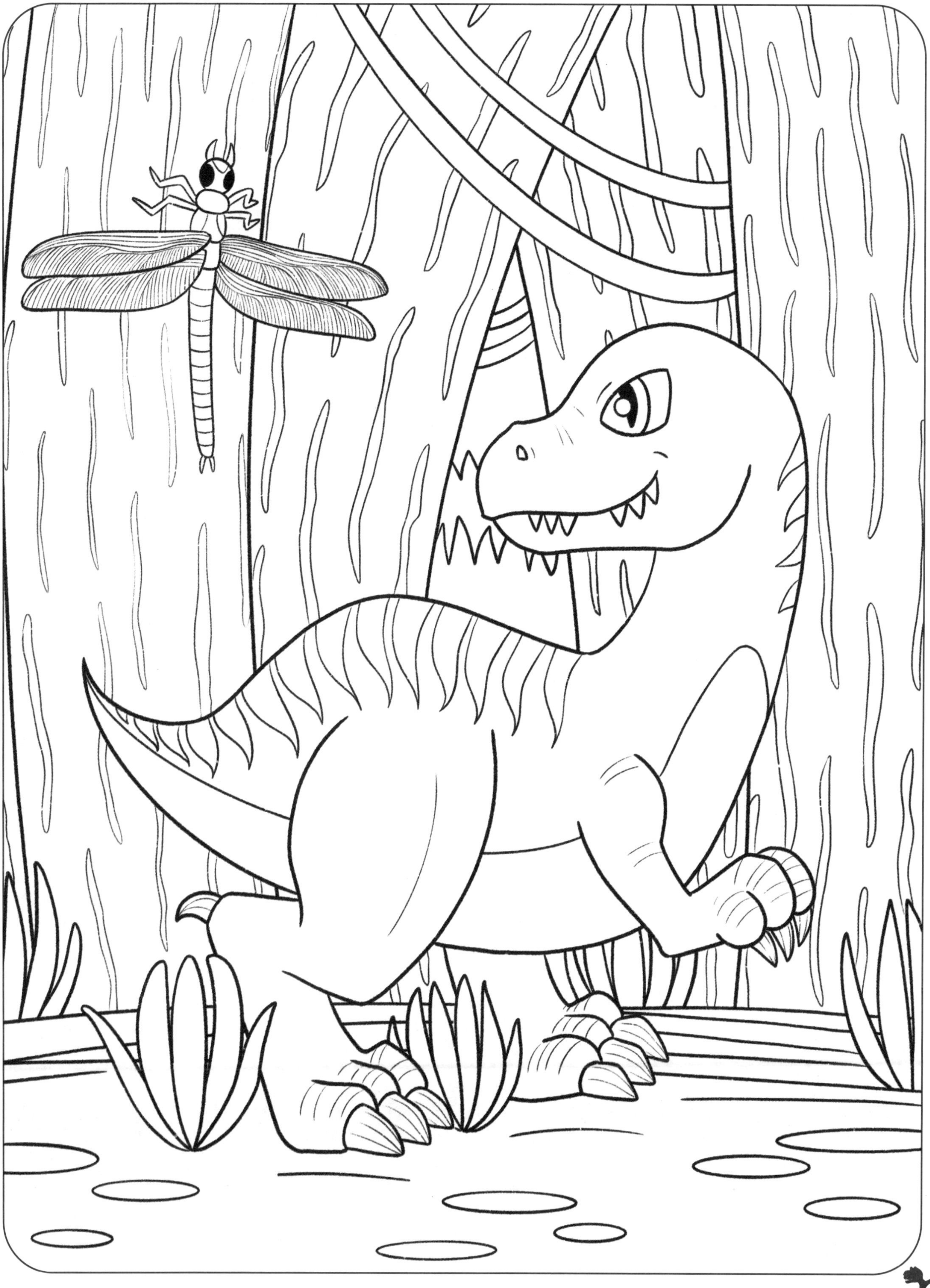

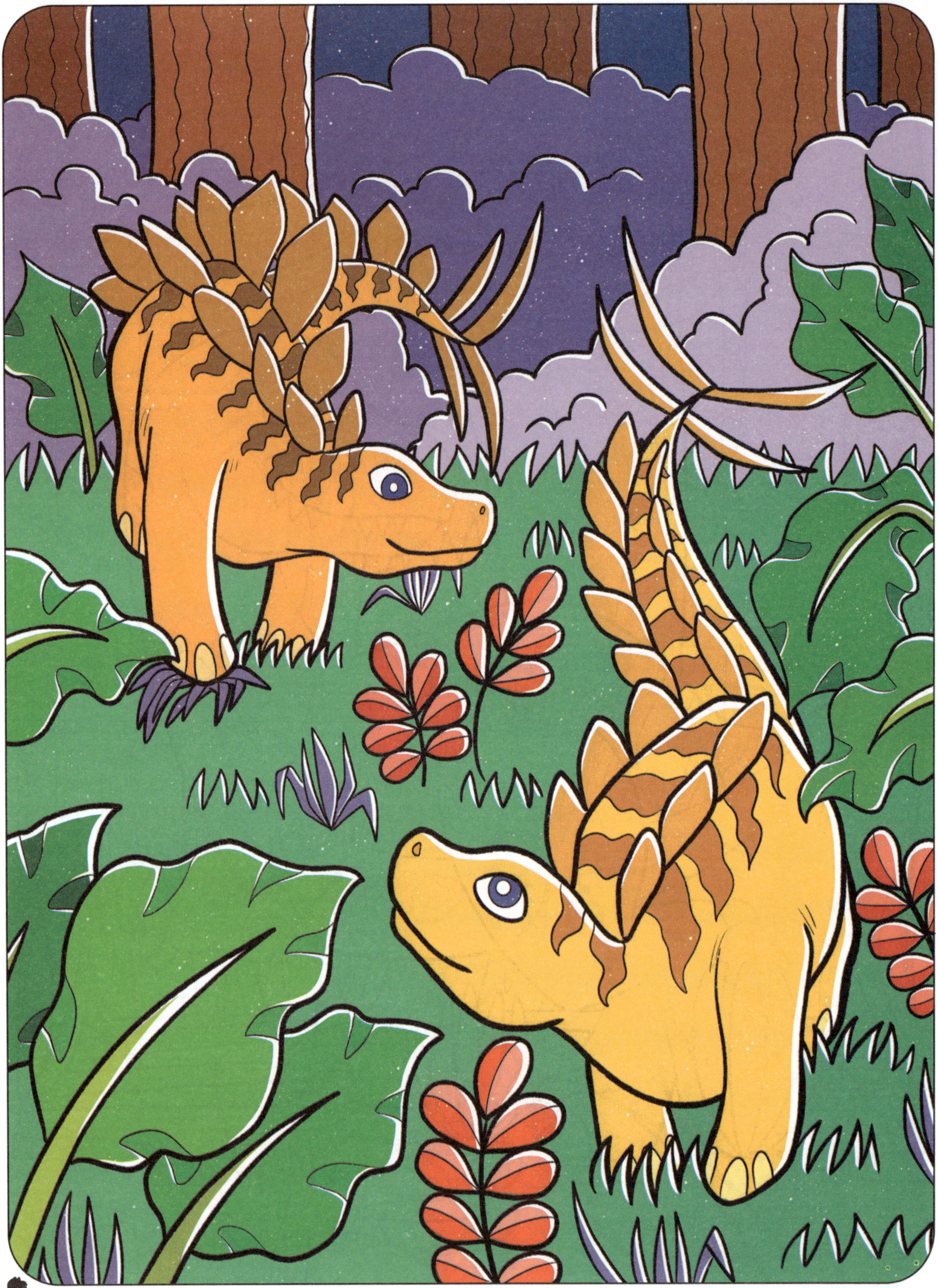

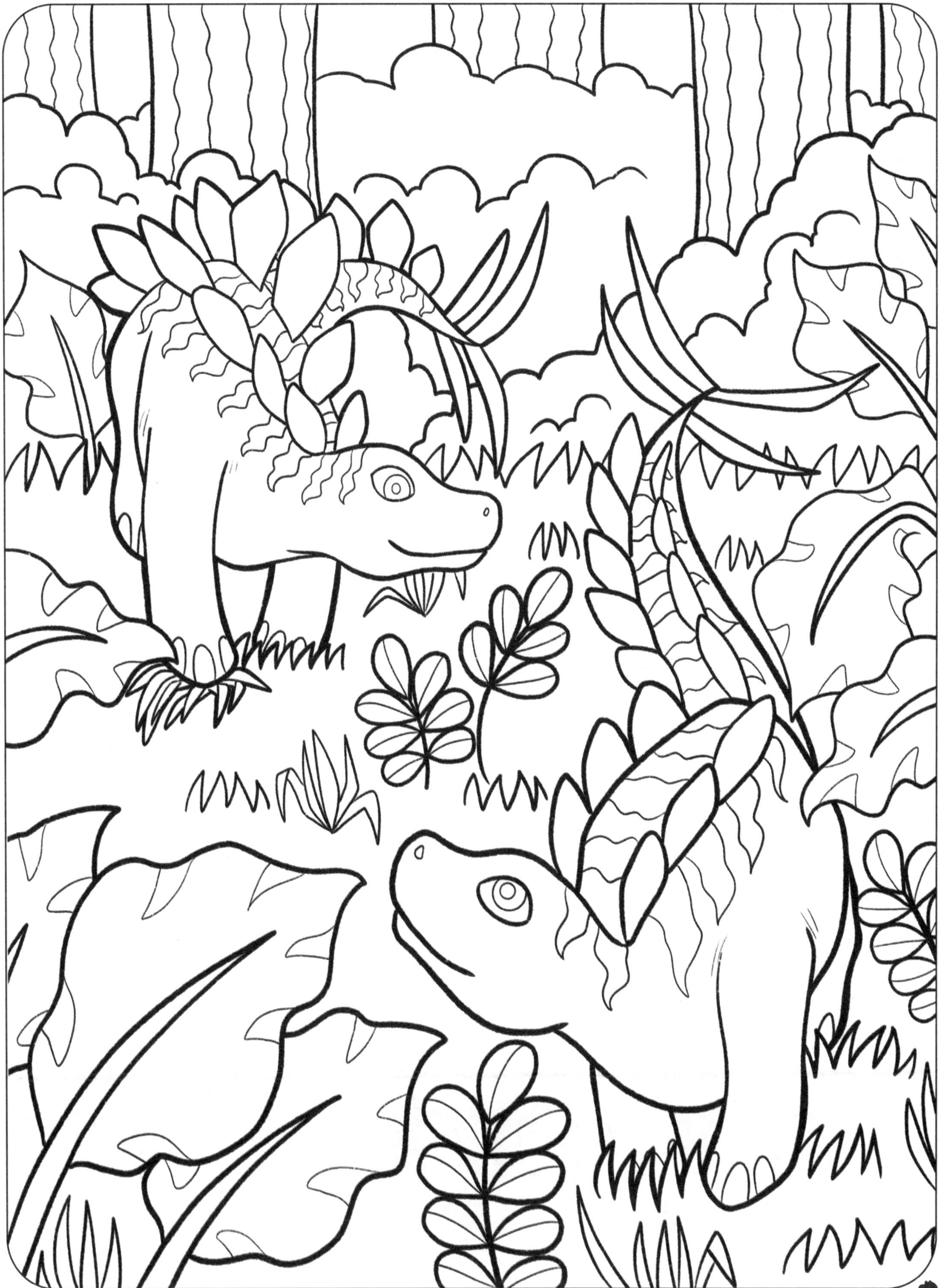

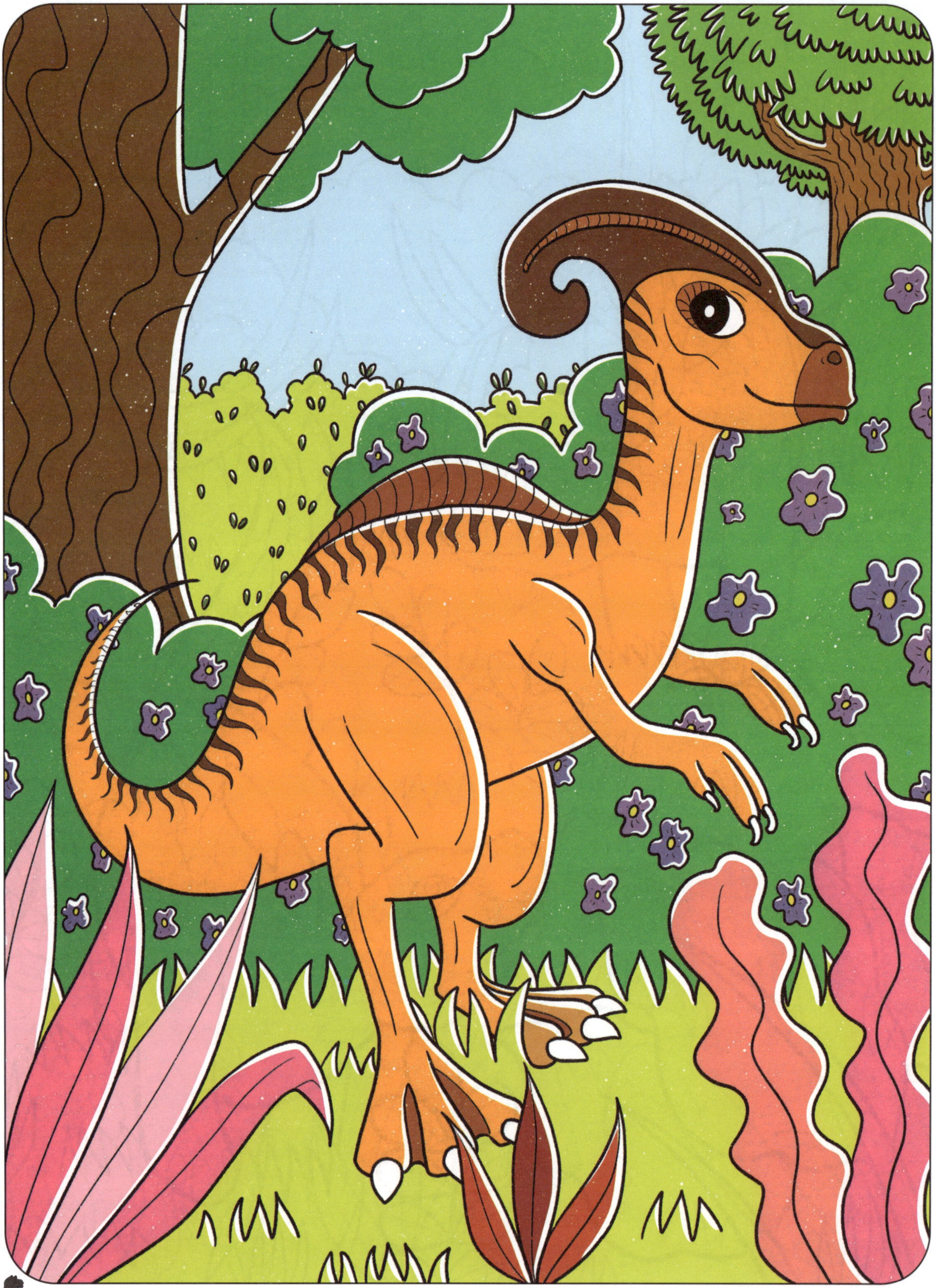

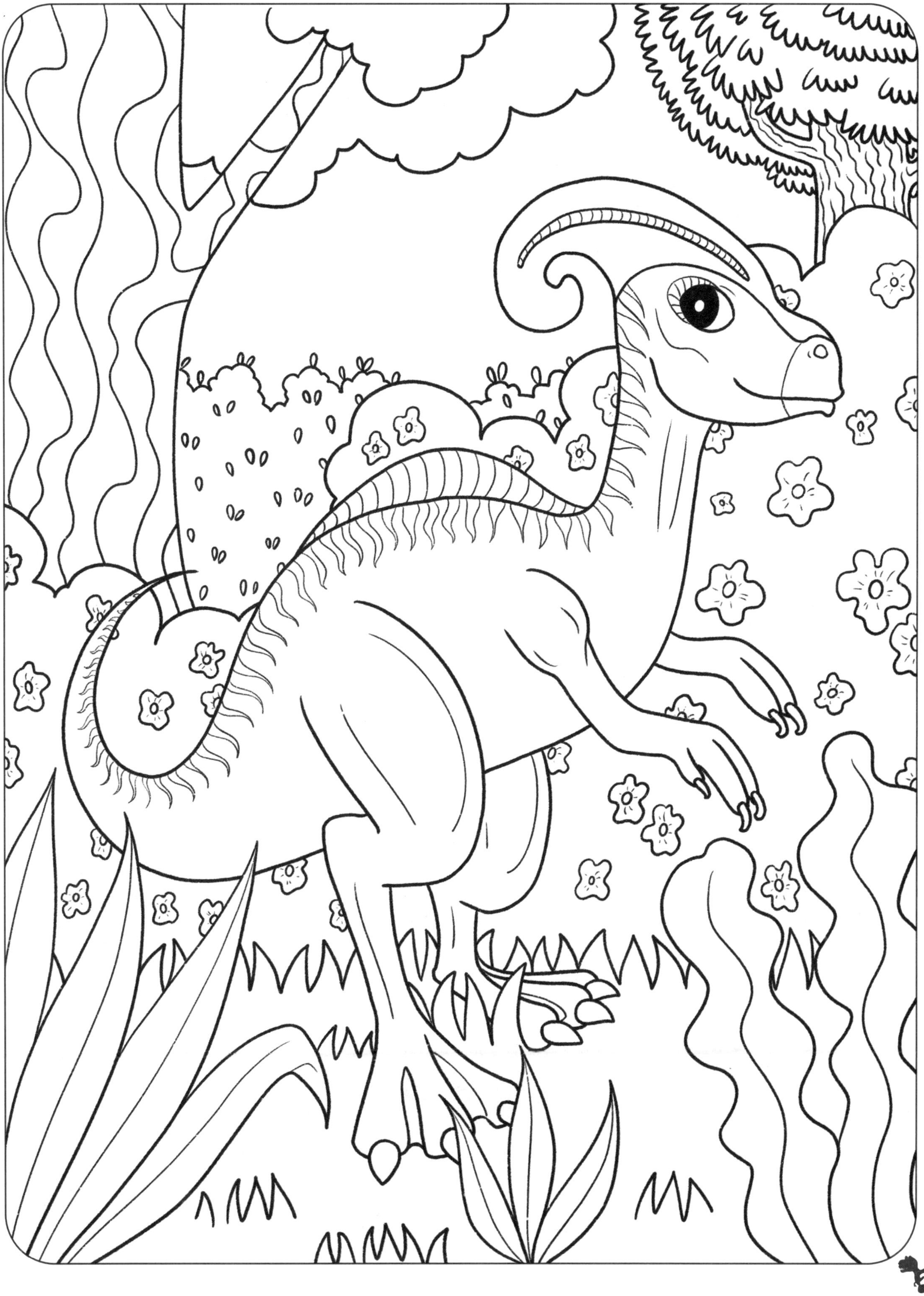

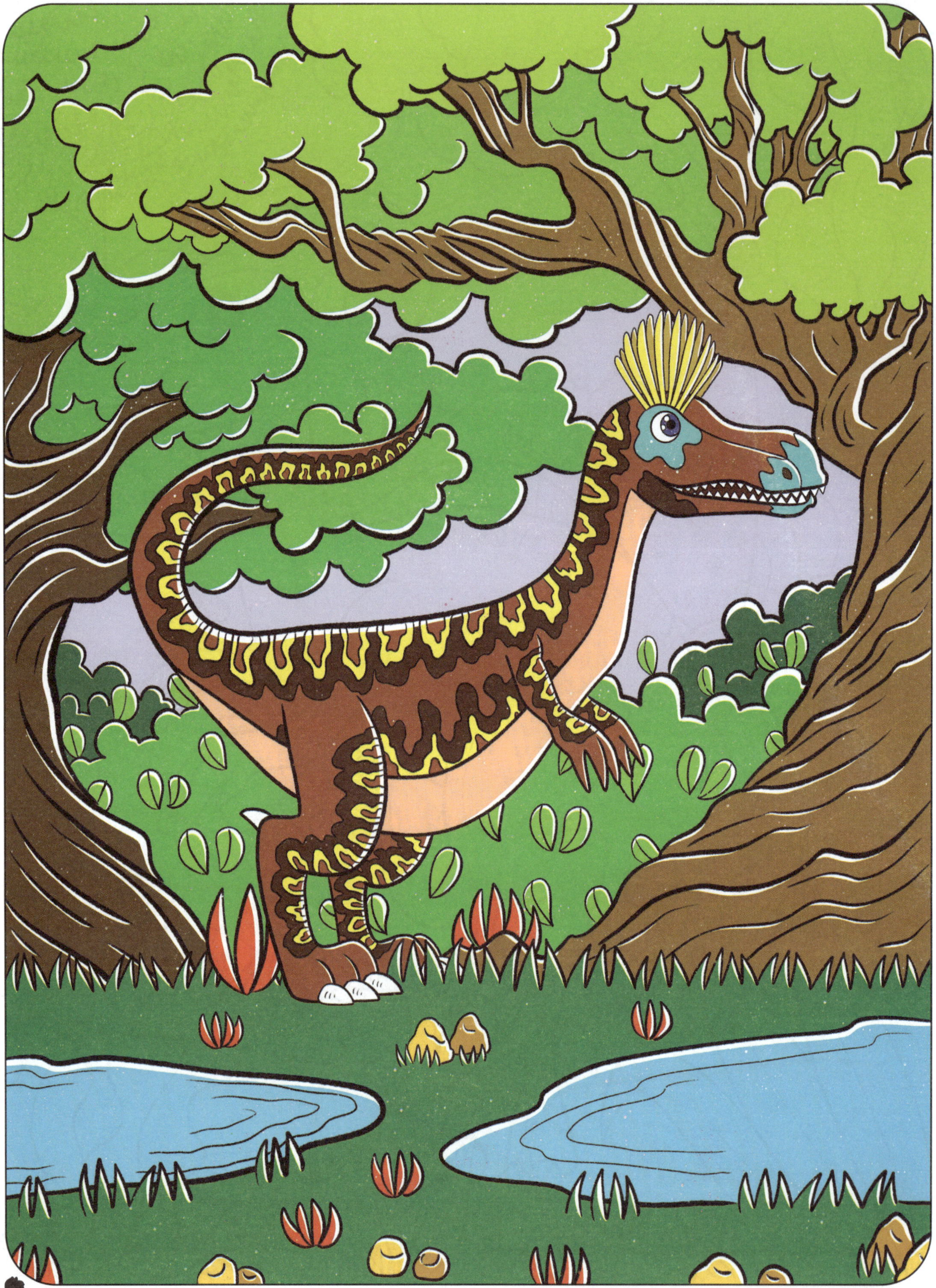

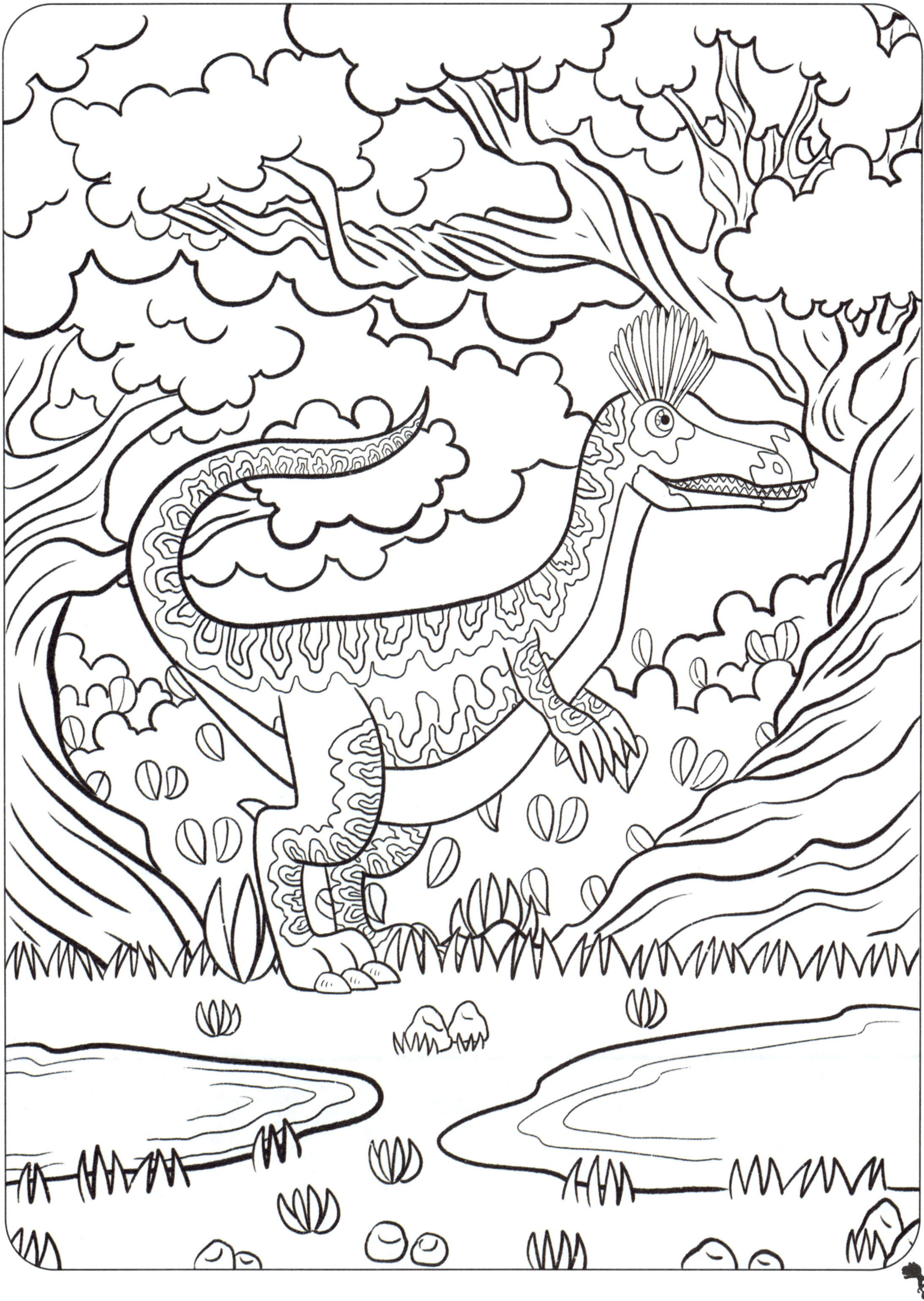

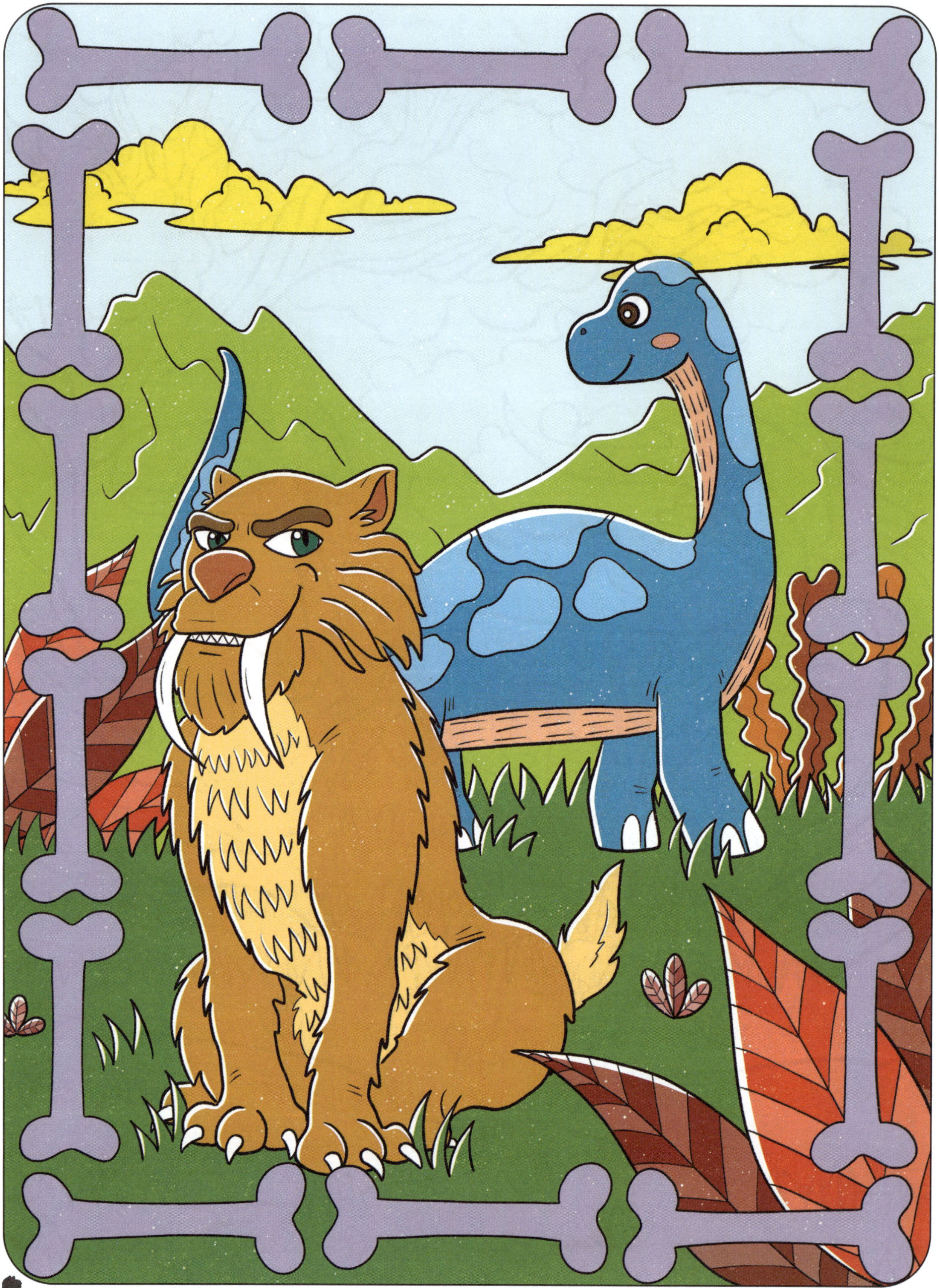

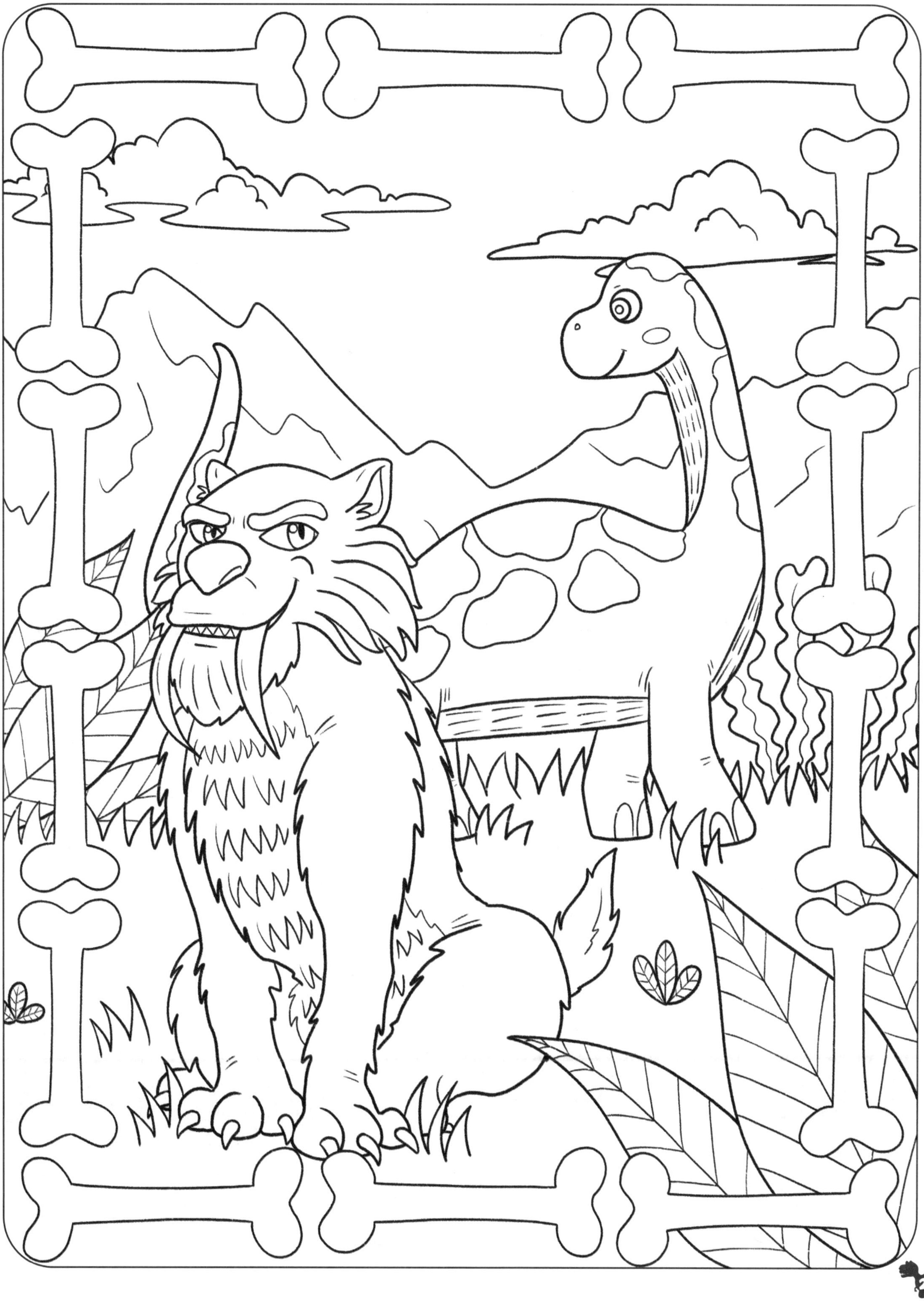

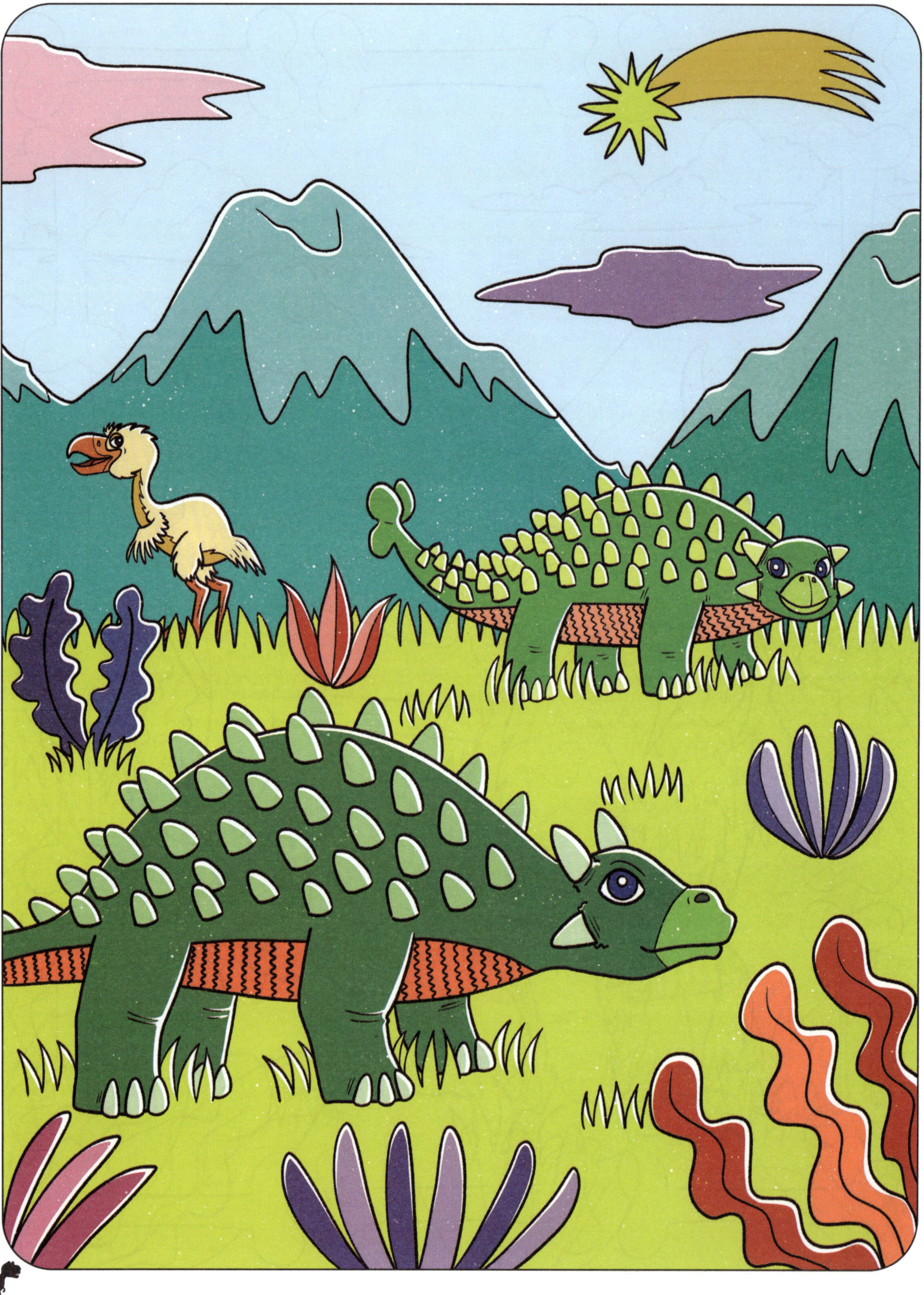

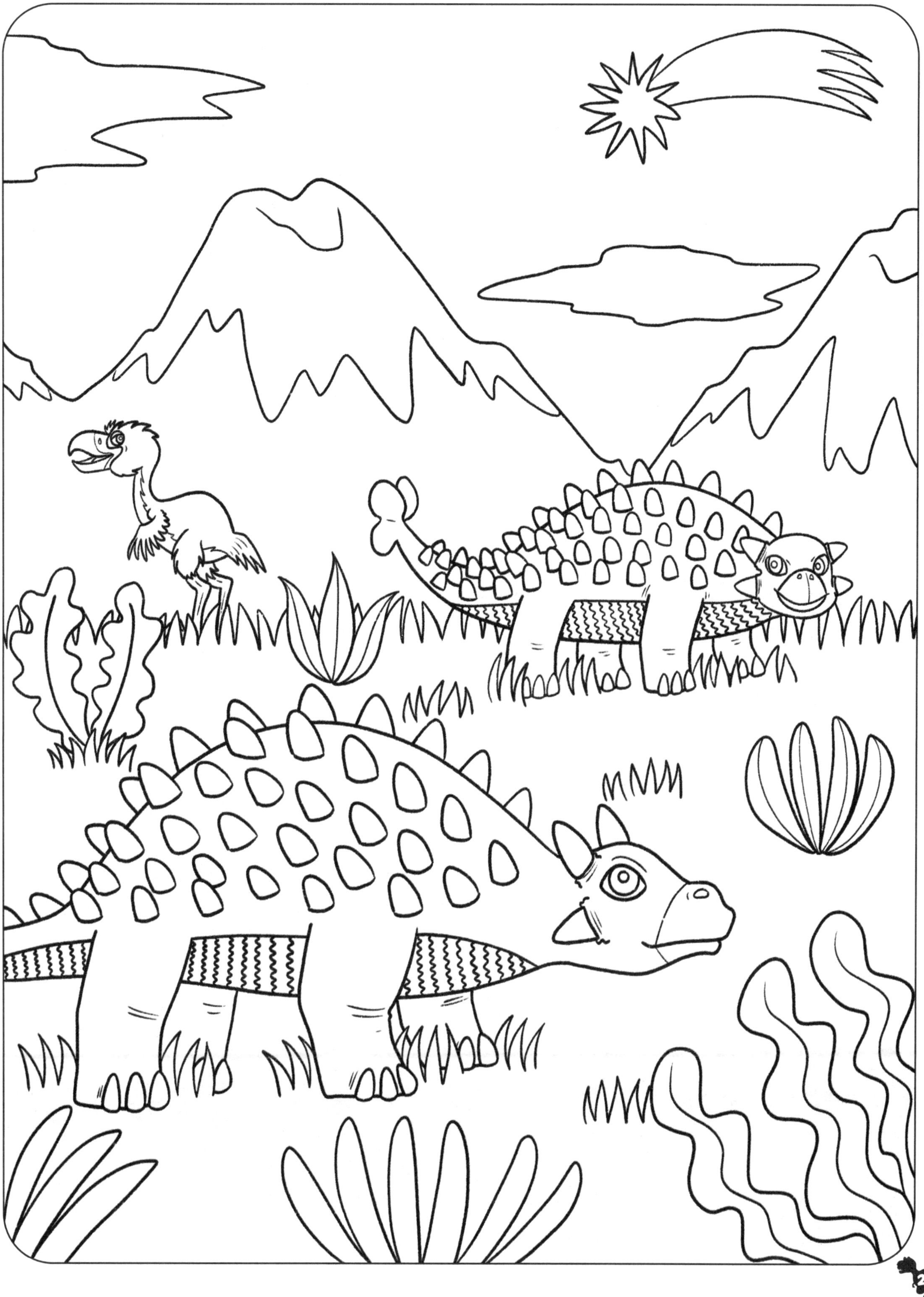

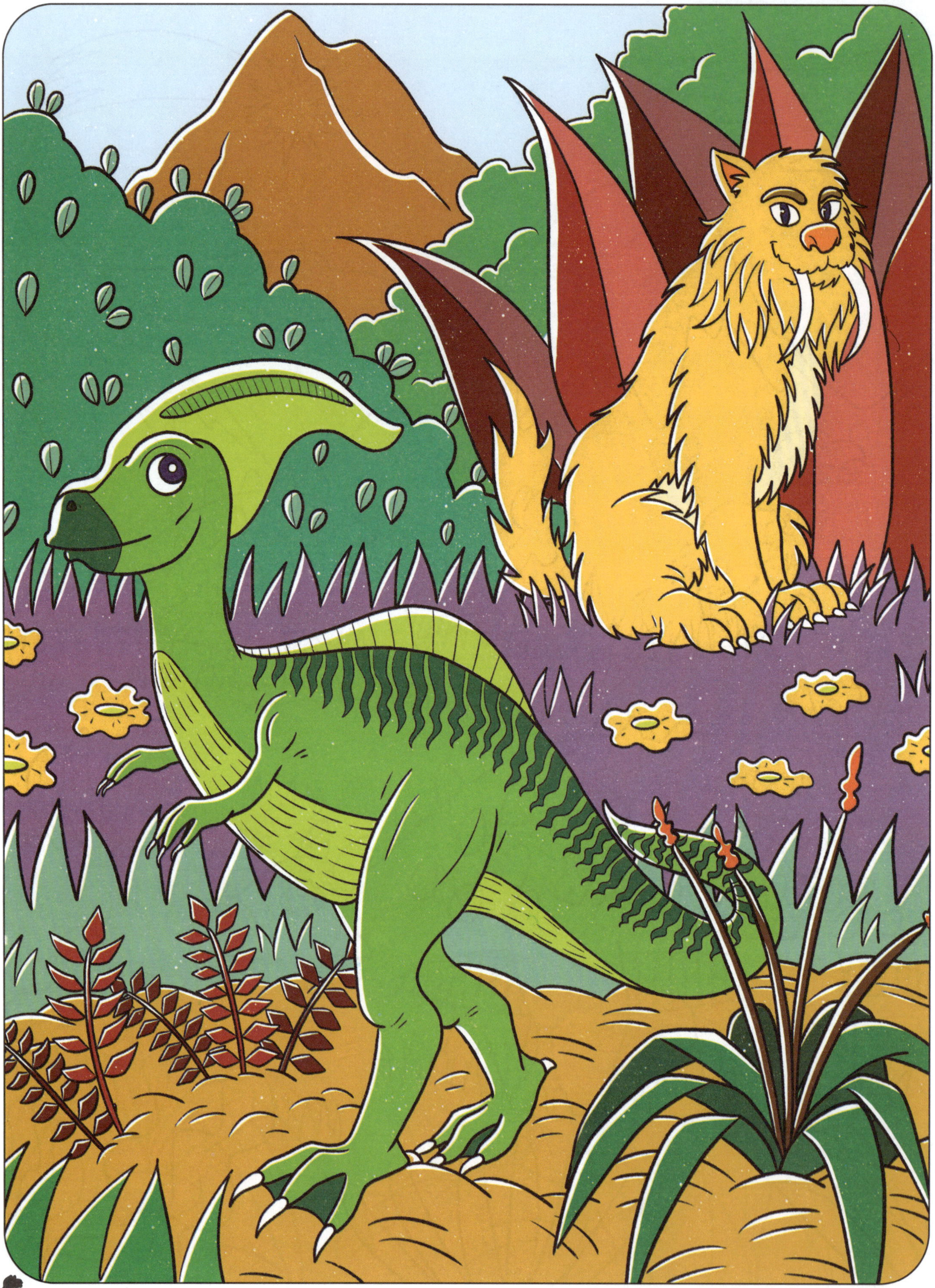

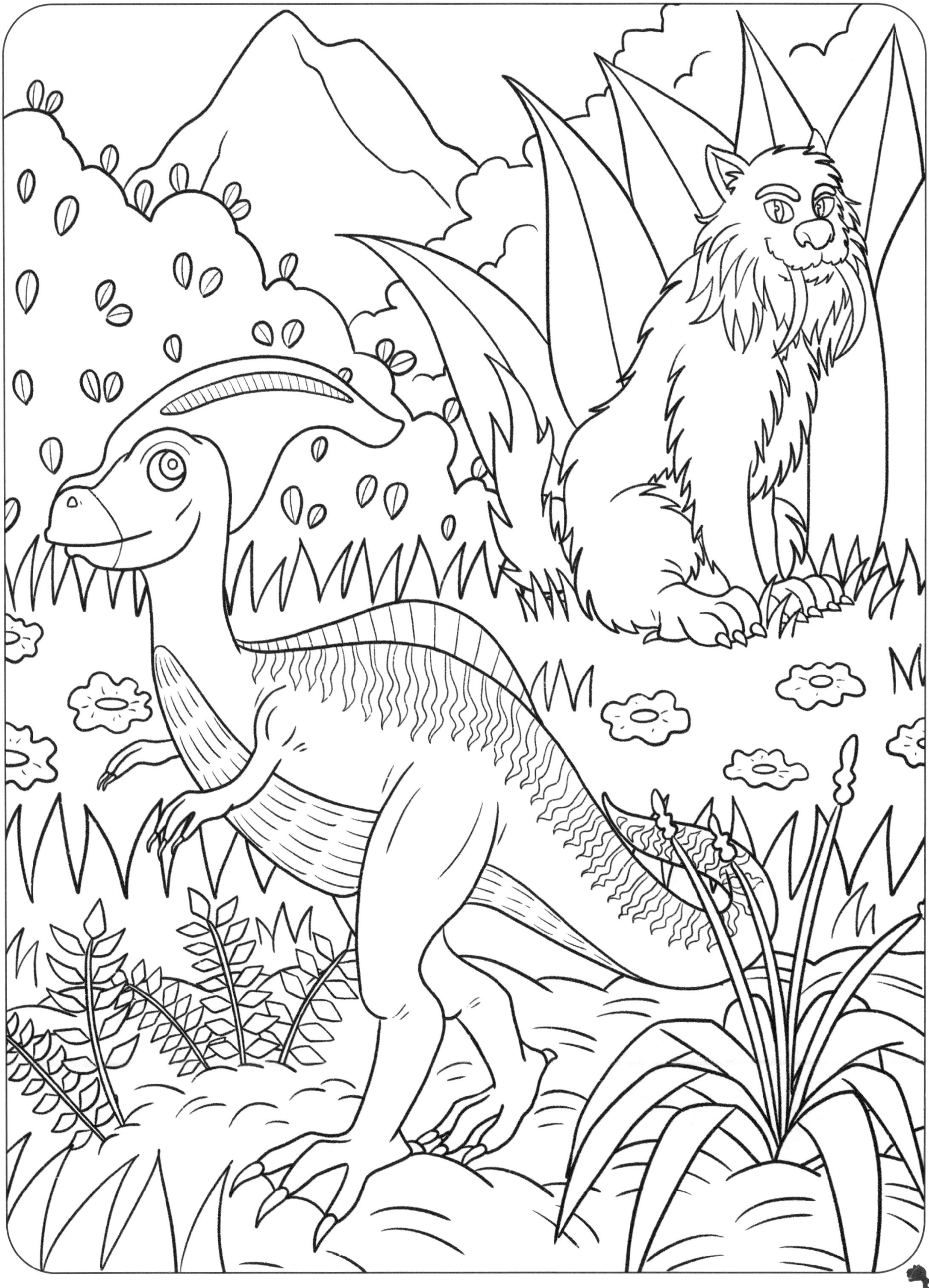

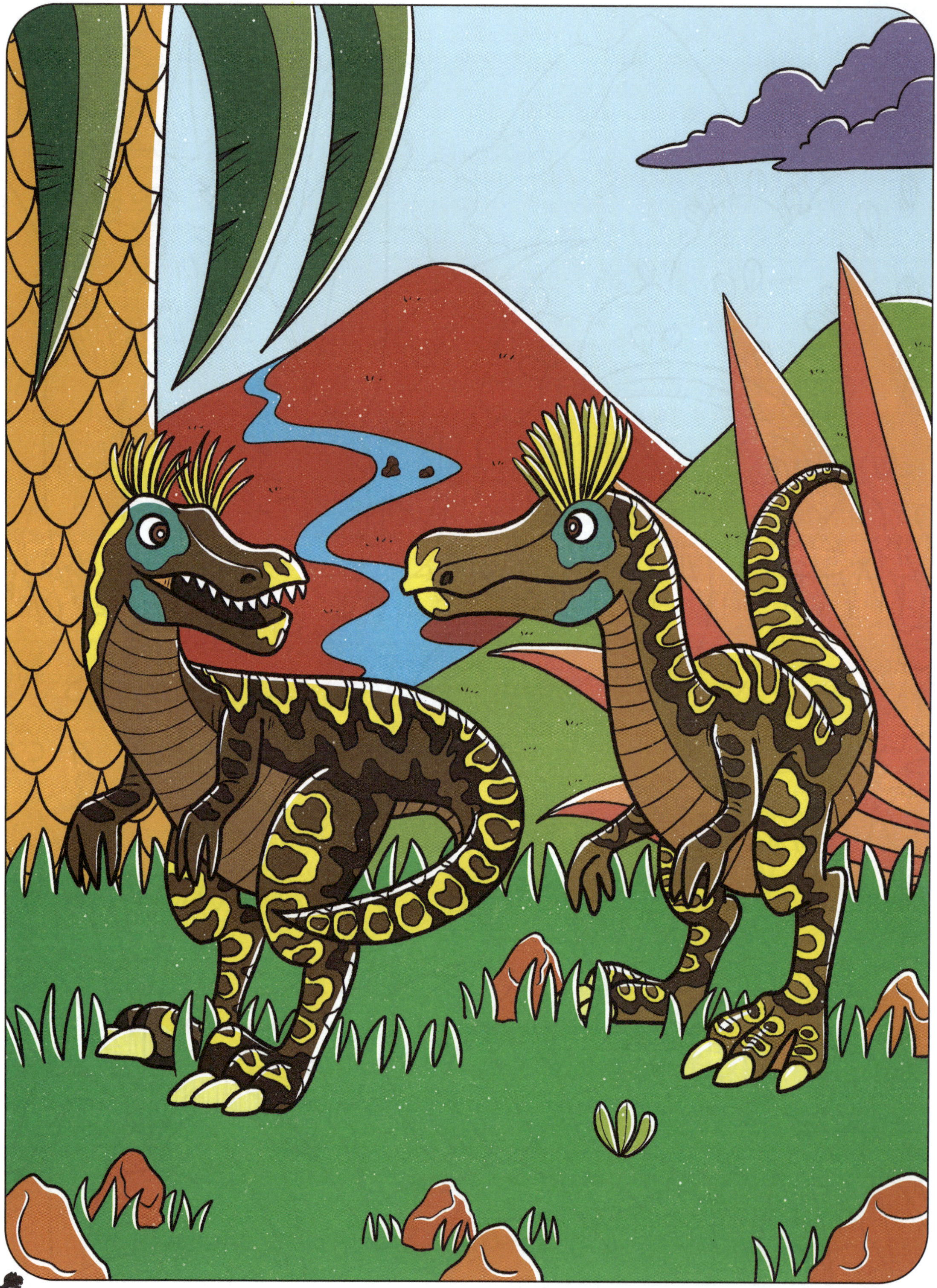

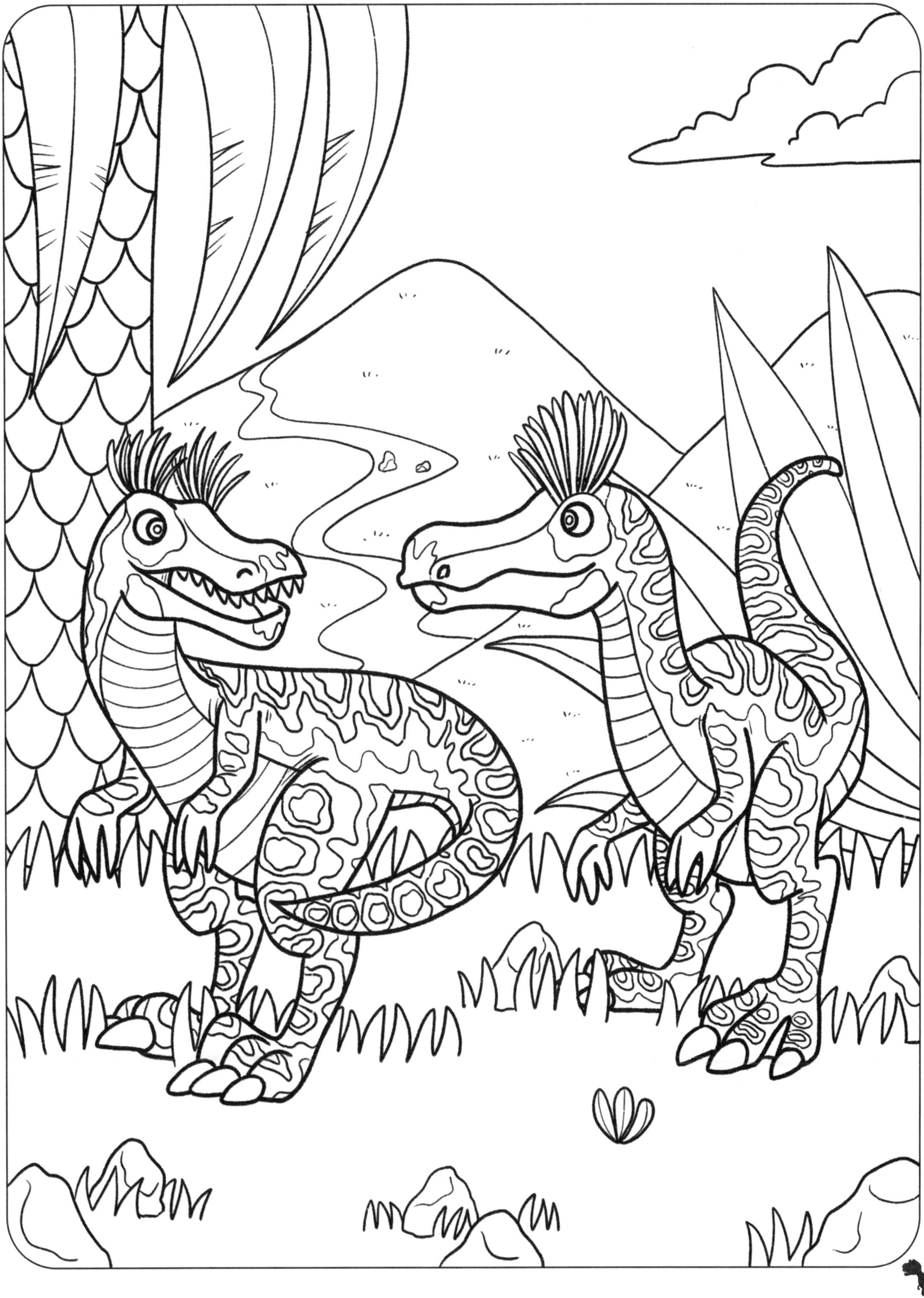

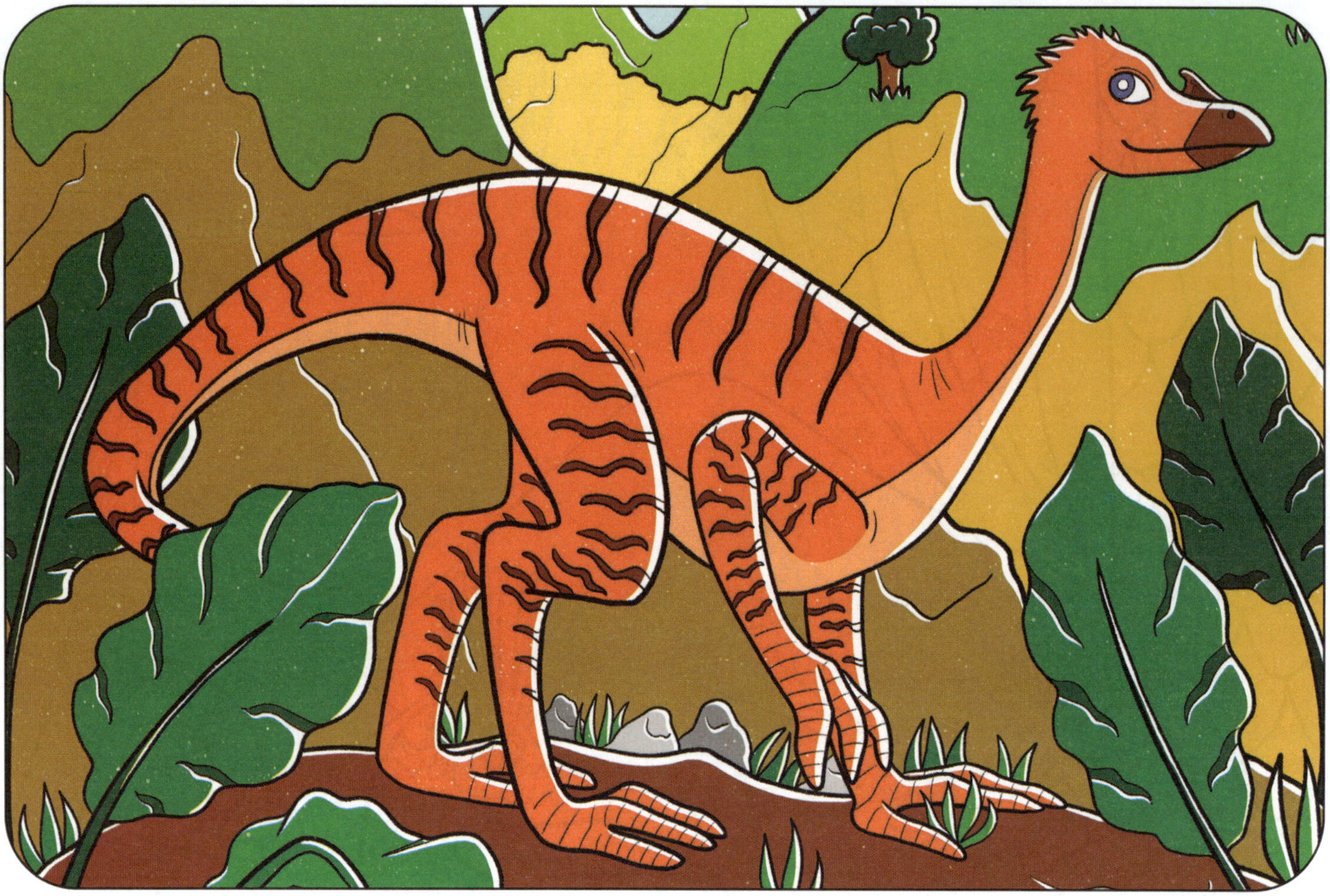

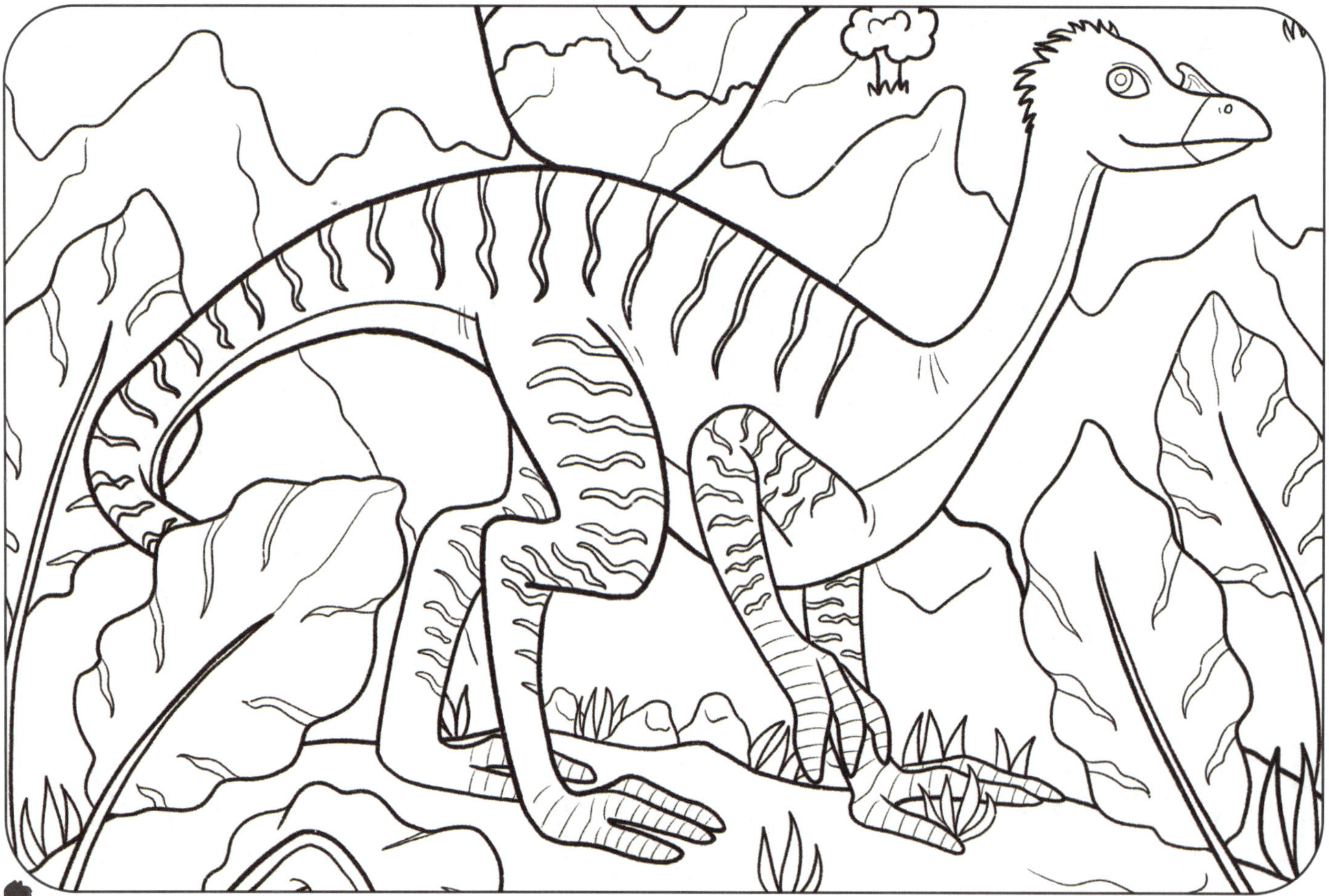